Easy Reading

Finding Joy and Meaning in Words

Laura Rose

Zephyr
Press ®

REACHING THEIR HIGHEST POTENTIAL

Tucson, Arizona

Easy Reading
Finding Joy and Meaning in Words

Grades: K–8

Printed in the United States of America

ISBN 1-56976-119-1

Editor: Rebecca Cook
Cover design: Daniel Miedaner
Design and production: Sheryl Shetler and Daniel Miedaner
Illustration: Kathleen Koopman, Sheryl Shetler, and Crystal Karl

Published by
Zephyr Press
P.O. Box 66006
Tucson, AZ 85728-6006
http://zephyrpress.com
http://giftsforteachers.com

Library of Congress Cataloging-in-Publication Data

Rose, Laura, 1942-
    Easy reading : finding joy and meaning in words / Laura Rose.
        p. cm.
    Includes bibliographical references.
    ISBN 1-56976-119-1 (alk. paper)
    1. Reading (Elementary)—Handbooks, manuals, etc. 2. Reading—Aids and devices—Handbooks, manuals, etc. 3. Visualization—Study and teaching (Elementary)—Handbooks, manuals, etc. I. Title.

LB1573.39 .R66 2000
372.4—dc21

00-033401

Contents

Foreword

Most "instruction" in reading can be placed into one of two categories: what to do in order to get ready to read, and what to do after you have finished.

Getting ready: You can review your prior knowledge, look at the title, and predict what will happen, or you can learn the "hard" words written on the chalkboard.

When you are done: Answer the teacher's questions, draw a picture of your favorite part, or fill in the blanks on a worksheet.

Precious little advice is offered to the novice reader as to what to do during the act of reading. The before-and-after-but-not-during approach is an example of what Janet Emig has called *magical thinking*. The novice reader is expected to read as if by magic (1983).

There are good reasons for our collective reluctance to offer what-to-do-in-your-head advice. We have only recently begun to understand how readers read; and we have barely begun to understand how we understand.

One consistent finding in the research literature is that many good thinkers and good readers visualize as they think or read. A few gifted individuals, many of whom are children, have the capacity to form *eidetic images*—mental visualizations that can be reexamined for detail the way the rest of us might reexamine a picture in a book. For most of us the images are fleeting and unstable. Despite their transitory nature, they are important.

Authors of narrative fiction make repeated use of description in introducing characters, depicting a setting, or explicating action. To fully understand the author's art, the reader must undertake to create visual images evoked by the written text.

The way in which readers people the novels they read with their own images makes reading a much more personal activity than watching images on a screen. When we watch a movie version of a story, we are at the mercy of the film director's imagination. When we read, we direct.

The same capacity for mental imagery is important in reading nonfiction. The sensitive reader will take Judy Donnelly's simple words, as she describes the last hours of the *Titanic*, and rage at the uncaring arrogance, bemoan the stupefying ignorance, and mourn the pointless deaths of the poor and powerless. "Many passengers are far from the lifeboats. They are the poor ones. Their rooms are down below. They know there is trouble too. But they do not know where to go. A few try to find their way. They go upstairs and down halls. Some are helped by seamen. Most just wait below" (Donnelly 1987).

Reading is more than mouthing the words accurately. It has nothing to do with getting someone else's questions right. It is breathing life into cold print. It is raising and seeking answers to your own questions. Skilled readers regard the printed words as a musical score; they provide the orchestra, the instruments, the interpretation, and the orchestration themselves. Some children can't do this. If we fill their days with letter/sound correspondences and irrelevant questions, then they never will.

Laura Rose does the educational community a great service. She takes the findings of arcane research studies and translates them into classroom practice. The researchers who do the research know much about mental imagery and little about teaching. Teachers know much about teaching and little about mental imagery. Laura Rose knows about them both. She brings them together in such a way as to offer teachers a truly unique addition to their instructional repertoire. She shows teachers how to offer novices advice as to what they might do while they are reading.

T.W. Johnson
Professor of Education
University of Victoria
British Columbia

Introduction

Great News!

You can significantly improve your students' comprehension, enjoyment, and personal involvement in reading at any grade level by using the simple series of clearly designed lessons provided in this manual. Hundreds of teachers in regular classrooms and reading support programs have had excellent results by using these strategies to teach their students how to add vivid mental pictures to their reading.

I regularly hear from teachers that with all the changes they have made in the way they teach their students reading over the last twenty years, the one thing that they refuse to give up is the visualization exercises they learned in my workshops. The reason they have retained these exercises is that after they've used them in their classrooms, they can see immediate and lasting improvement in their students' enthusiasm for reading. Reading teachers send me letters documenting the progress in years of reading growth their students have made after just a few months of using this program. In addition to strong anecdotal evidence, many formal research studies have also documented significant gains in both comprehension and recall when students are taught how to use visualization to bring their reading fully to life (Gambrell, Kapinus, and Wilson 1997; Borduin and Charles 1994; Olson and Gee 1991).

If Visualization Is So Terrific, Why Don't We Hear More about It?

If you read "official" lists of comprehension strategies, visualization will almost always be affirmed, as it is in the newest intensively skills-based California Reading Framework (California State Board of Education 1999) and in most college reading textbooks. In Howard Gardner's seven intelligences (Gardner 1983), visualization is an integral part of the visual/spatial intelligence and plays a supporting role in some others as well, such as intrapersonal intelligence. Researchers who study brain activity with sophisticated medical machinery such as PET scans (Chugani 1996) have recently found evidence that contrary to earlier notions that visualizing is solely a right-brain function, the entire brain is more active during visualization than in nearly any other single thinking activity (Bruer 1999). Some researchers imply that engaging a child's brain in this kind of stimulation can lead to added dendrite formation and actual growth in ultimate brain potential (Sylwester 1995).

There is currently strong and ever-growing support for constructivist teaching strategies, an educational paradigm where students are regarded as intelligent beings whose job is to bring meaning to their own world. The teacher's job therefore is not to "drill and kill," but to provide students with a rich, stimulating environment in which to ask questions and investigate the answers. Using visualization to teach reading comprehension is the ultimate in constructivism. It affirms that most students can essentially teach themselves how to read if they are provided with enough encouragement and the proper tools to make personal meaning out of what they are reading.

An enthusiastic blending of the creative arts with standard curriculum regularly shows a significant effect on learning even on very standard measures (Sautter 1994). One explanation of this comes from brain researchers like Elaine de Beauport (1996), who suggests that the arts add a visualization component to content areas. For example, by adding music, dance, and drawing to math, she found that students were able to visualize equations and numbers. De Beauport claims to have banished learning disabilities at her school by using these methods.

With all this success, why are there so few programs that offer teachers the support they need to teach this vital comprehension strategy? Perhaps the reason is that most teachers are active readers and therefore active visualizers, so it is difficult for them to even entertain the notion that some of their students cannot create mental pictures in their minds' eyes. Even though repeated research does demonstrate that when children visualize, their comprehension increases, few teachers are aware that unless we specifically model and remind our students to visualize, they rarely do so (Gambrell, Kapinus, and Wilson 1987).

Research conducted by Project Mind's Eye, a Title IV C Project in Escondido, California (1979), disclosed that approximately one out of five students in every classroom *cannot* close their eyes and "see" even a simple apple or banana, let alone imagine the detailed scenery and rich characters from books such as *Treasure Island* (Robert Louis Stevenson 1883) or *Where the Red Fern Grows* (Wilson Rawls 1961). Small wonder that adults who have not developed the skill of visualization often readily admit they do not like to read anything but "how-to" manuals and exclusively factual information. Teacher after teacher has confirmed to me that the very students who cannot create a mental picture are the same students who do not succeed at reading.

Second- and third-grade teachers are aware of the tremendous difficulty in convincing some students to shift from picture books to chapter books. This reluctance can be easily understood if we stop to consider that the students who are most resistant to this shift may be the same students who are unskilled at creating mental pictures. For these students, books filled with banks of words on every page present a very intimidating proposition indeed.

But What about Phonics?

There is currently a great emphasis on phonemic awareness and phonics to teach beginning reading. The research quoted by the leaders in this movement is questionable on several counts and hotly contested by other excellent researchers (Smith 1999). Let's stipulate, however, that many students do find phonics helpful in learning to read. It has been an element of my reading programs during twenty years of teaching kindergarten through grade 8. In my current role of conducting student-teaching methods classes at a state university, I strongly encourage my students to master these approaches. Even so, phonics can only take us so far on the road to reading and no further. Unless we can bring meaning to the word we decode, the sentence that includes that word will be meaningless.

"I walked into the kitchen and there on the table was the dreaded *rinktumditty* just staring at me with its one yellow eye." Now I'm sure that you were able to read every word in that sentence and to decode the "rinktumditty," but just saying the word did not tell you what it looks, feels, smells, sounds or tastes like. It isn't until I tell you that a rinktumditty is a square of toast with a hole where an egg is poached that you get the mental picture. Whatever other strategies students use to learn how to read, they must create mental pictures from the printed words before they can truly comprehend.

I call it the "chicken soup for the mind" theory: An author has a vision for a story, just as a cook creates fabulous, one-of-a-kind chicken soup. The soup can't be shipped through the mail to you, so the cook takes all the water out of it—dehydrates it—and makes instant chicken-soup mix. This can be sent through the mail, just as an author can send dull, dry letters to you through a book. The chicken soup tastes just awful unless water is added, and the book has no flavor at all unless the reader adds imagination to bring the story fully back to life. This is the role of visualization. It enables the reader to recreate, with a personal flair, the marvelous "chicken soup" conceived by the author, and to eat it all up with gusto. Phonics alone cannot turn the dried flakes into yummy chicken soup. Letters do not make the story—imagination does.

There is additional concern over intensive phonics programs for at-risk readers. Often the lower readers are given extra helpings of phonics, which may or may not be beneficial to all students. The time dedicated to these lessons must come from somewhere in the school day, and often they come during the time when other students are actually reading. This then poses a problem, since the one activity that everyone agrees will increase reading skills of all kinds is time spent really reading. The one-two punch of an overemphasis on phonics and a deficiency of real reading time has been dubbed the basic skills conspiracy, which demands: "First you have to get the words right and the facts straight before you can get to the *what ifs* or *I wonders.*" (Pearson 1993).

Of course, we need to teach phonics and other discrete reading skills. But, even more important, we must get our students reading—deeply, widely, and for long periods of time. If you teach your students to vividly and deliberately visualize as they read, they will begin to enjoy and understand their reading more, and, best of all, they will want to read more.

Visualizing is perhaps the only thing we can teach students to do that will help them make greater sense of what they read *while they are actually reading.* Every other comprehension strategy tells our students what to do before or after they read. Visualization is the most powerful strategy children can employ while they are in the middle of the reading process, which is where we want them to spend most of their reading time.

Should I Use This Approach Only with My Poorer Readers?

I developed this approach with my lowest readers in mind. However, the program can be used effectively with students of different reading abilities. Several years after the publication of my original *Picture This* manual, I was delighted to find that it was chosen by the National Javitts Project for English-Language Arts Research as an exemplary program for gifted education.

In my classroom, I have watched nearly every student enjoy the exercises that develop visualization skills and, consequently, enjoy more than ever their daily reading. I said earlier that one out of five students doesn't visualize at all. Another one out of five visualizes all the time, with no help from you whatsoever. The other three can visualize, but they do not usually do it while reading unless you give them regular encouragement (Escondido Union School District 1979). If you engage all of your students in this program, you will see an appreciable increase in reading enjoyment, reading volume, and reading comprehension. This approach goes beyond mere reward systems to encourage more reading through greater intrinsic reading enjoyment, and more reading inevitably leads to better reading (Pearson 1993).

Does This Approach Work for Students at All Grade Levels?

This program has been used very successfully by hundreds of teachers from kindergarten through grade 6 in regular classrooms and reading pull-out programs. This manual is designed so that both primary and upper-grade teachers can use it easily. My workshops have been particularly well received by special education teachers, both because of its effectiveness and its ability to be used with children of many different ages. It is very workable in mixed-grade classrooms as well.

Can I Really Help Some of My Poorest Readers in the Intermediate Grades to Pull Ahead in Reading?

Studies have been bombarding us lately with the news that once children fall below grade level it is extremely rare for them ever to catch up. There is no single system, they tell us, that "works" to give new hope to poorer readers (Flippo 1999). Even with the great emphasis nationwide on reading improvement, about one-third of our students do not learn to read competently during the primary years, and gains in reading competence after students reach grades 4–12 are rare (Joyce 1999). Success has been documented, however, for visualization techniques (Bell 1986; Escondido Union School District 1979; Gambrell, Kapinus, and Wilson 1987; Olson and Gee 1991).

Studies done by the *Mind's Eye* project in California yielded extremely positive results. After learning to visualize during reading, poorer readers in grades four and above were often able to make several years' growth. The year that I developed this program with my fifth graders, I saw for the first time a student who entered my classroom reading at the second-grade level transform himself into a student who was rarely seen without a Tarzan or a Louis L'Amour book tucked under his arm.

There are very few resources available to help lower readers after the third grade; neither phonics nor any other single method has a positive track record with these older students (Fielding and Pearson 1994). A recent article in *Educational Leadership* (Daniels, Zemelmen, and Bazar 1999) reviews decades of research in reading methods and reminds us that when low-achieving students have been removed from heavily phonics-based programs and immersed in literature (read-alouds, memorization of favorite stories; i.e., the kinds of exercises you will find in this manual) they make significant gains (Chomsky 1978).

So, why not make room in your reading program for a system that is not only research-based, but positive, engaging, and that affirms the inner ability of your students to learn what makes sense to them? You and your students will enjoy reading as never before as their comprehension increases in a meaning-centered, literature-rich environment.

How to Use This Manual

This manual offers the following two options for teaching students to increase their reading competence and enjoyment by learning to visualize while they read.

The Sensory Method

First, the most exciting and effective option is to use the series of lessons in Section I: Developing the Mind's Eye. It starts students visualizing without print. Students develop visualization through an engaging variety of sensory and memory activities, or "Journeys," until their skills are sure and strong (about two weeks in the primary grades and four weeks in grades 4–8). Section II: Reading with the Mind's Eye then adds the print component by developing visualization of a folk tale over a two-week period of lessons. Further links are made between reading and visualization throughout section II and section III. Writing with the Mind's Eye shows you how to enrich your students' writing by using visualization strategies.

There are several strong advantages to this total approach:

- For younger children it is a playful, natural path that agrees with constructivist and developmental philosophies.

- Older students who are discouraged learners become engaged in activities that do not seem like the usual "reading" and "writing" exercises they have grown to dread and, therefore, try to avoid.

- We begin right where the students are. At the beginning they are merely asked to do something that all children can do—remember some good experiences from their earlier years. As the students' mental imaging skills increase with each new exercise, they find themselves reading and writing with greater comprehension and creativity.

- The program can be done with your entire class or with a small group of students, or even with individual students in a pull-out program.

- Students of all ages and ability levels enjoy the activities.

- Brain research suggests that stimulation of the brain may actually facilitate the growth of neural connectors and add to ultimate brain potential (Thompson 1998; Sylwester 1982).

The Direct Link to Print Method

The second possible pathway to reading with visualization is to start directly with Section II: Reading with the Mind's Eye, which involves students immediately with print. Daily, students read a short passage from a story, and you ask them a series of questions about their mental images. These probing, repetitive visualization questions help students begin regularly visualizing as they read. Skipping right to section II has several potential advantages:

- With older children in particular, it may be easier for parents and administration to understand and support the program, because it looks more like traditional schoolwork. If you teach in a situation where sensory input and blindfolds might be misunderstood or even discouraged, then you might want to choose, at least initially, this second option.

- If parents in your district have expressed objections to the classroom use of visualization due to religious beliefs, this option avoids activities that might make these parents feel spiritually uncomfortable while still teaching their children the mental skills they need to fully develop their reading comprehension and creative writing.

How Does This Program Fit into My School Year?

This program is not meant to replace the successful teaching strategies you are presently using in your classroom. Instead, it is intended as a supplement to your current methods, with the specific goal of increasing reading comprehension and enjoyment for every student in your classroom and giving your discouraged readers a fresh chance to learn the true meaning of reading.

You can introduce this program at any time during the school year. Allow a period a day for four to six weeks to fully develop visualization skills in all your students. The time that it will take is more than justified by the greater depth of reading comprehension and enjoyment your students will experience for the rest of the year and, quite possibly, for the rest of their lives.

Once your students are all visualizing on a regular basis, one or two lessons each week will encourage and further develop visualization skills. You can regularly revisit any of the exercises in Section I: Developing the Mind's Eye to keep their minds' eyes alert and creative, or continue on to the lessons offered in Section II: Reading with the Mind's Eye and Section III: Writing with the Mind's Eye.

Note: Keep in mind that grades 4 through 8 should spend more time with the pre-print activities since there will likely be some deeply discouraged readers in this group who need to participate in some confidence-building exercises.

Suggested Schedule for Teaching Visualization Skills

Week 1 All Grade Levels
Chapter 1, Sensory Memories: 5 lessons

Week 2 All Grade Levels
Chapter 2, Best Memories: 2–3 lessons
Chapter 3, Listen My Children: 2–3 lessons

Week 3–4 Primary Grades
Section II–Reading with the Mind's Eye
Chapter 1, Image While You Read: 10 lessons over 2 weeks

Week 3 Grades 4–8
Chapter 4, Archetypes: 2 lessons
Chapter 5, Characters and Settings: 2–3 lessons

Week 4 Grades 4–8
Chapter 5, Characters and Settings: 2–3 more lessons
Chapter 6, Create a Myth: 2 lessons

Week 5–6 Grades 4–8
Section II–Reading with the Mind's Eye
Chapter 7, Image While You Read: 10 lessons over 2 weeks

Once your students are all visualizing while they read, any chapter can be used from any section.

Small Cautions

Allergies

These days many children have food allergies. Before any Journey where food is ingested, be sure to check to make sure that no student is allergic to the Journey's focus.

You can substitute a similar food for any student who has an allergy (e.g. a candy cane instead of peanut brittle if there is peanut allergy).

Unhappy Memories

Even though the memory exercises are designed to elicit pleasant memories, there may be instances where an unhappy memory is jogged, as can happen with any reading or writing activity. If this occurs, the opportunity to draw or write about the experience is usually a very appropriate avenue for the student to process and deal with feelings. It is important, however, not to require that such memories be shared with the class.

Use your own judgment in selecting the exercises that will best fit the needs of your particular students. For instance, if you know that one of your students had a very bad experience with water or near drowning, do not use the "Best Water Fun" exercise; instead, substitute another exercise from that chapter.

Important Hints to Optimize Success

For the first few lessons, there will probably be a few students who do not draw anything after the visualization exercise. When you ask them what they saw, they will probably say, "Nothing." This does not mean that you have done something wrong; these are precisely the non-visualizing students for whom this program was designed.

These students are the reason why these first exercises are all about early memories. Every child has memories, so we hope that a sensory cue such as a marshmallow, an orange slice or an ice cube can translate these pleasant early memories into visual images that can then be drawn on paper. You must find a way to actively engage these students, however. If you do not press the issue, they will sit and do nothing, and you will see no effect on their language arts skills. Here are several strategies that worked for me.

For Younger Students and Those Who Do Not Mind Being Touched by the Teacher

During the drawing period, go to each child individually and ask what he or she saw. If the students tell you, encourage them to sketch their ideas on their papers. Reward this effort.

If they say, "Nothing," pick up the sensory stimulus (for instance, a marshmallow) and repeat the suggestions from the visualization. You might rub the marshmallow across the back of the child's hand and say, "What does that remind you of? Is there any time that you felt something like this when you were younger?"

If there is still no response, give hints. "Did you ever pet an animal that felt like this? Or did you ever feel your mom's hand holding yours?"

Keep this up until they give any answer at all, and then say, "Great! Draw that!" Once they begin to draw, you can ask more questions about size, color, taste, and so on, to help the student more fully develop the image. You may need to repeat this extra help for several days, but soon the students will get the idea and do it without your intervention.

For Older Students and Those Who Do Not Wish to Be Touched by the Teacher in Front of Their Peers

Go to each student who is not drawing. Ask what each saw and, if the student can tell you, just encourage the drawing. If the student says, "Nothing," ask: "What color was the nothing?"

In my experience, the answer to this is often, "I don't know," which I take to mean, "I'm not playing this game, so how about leaving me alone?" I respond with, "Close your eyes and take a look," by which I mean, "No, I won't leave you alone because this is important schoolwork, but I will give you all the help you need and I won't go away until I get an answer because I care about your education."

Surprisingly, students' answer to the question of color is seldom "black" but more often is "gray" or even "red." This is a strong clue that this child is not visualizing, because gray or red is the color that you will see with your physical eyes through your eyelids, rather than the black of the mind's eye.

Whatever the answer, direct the students to draw that color, filling their papers fully. I express just as much pleasure with their product as with any other. After repeating this process for several days, students get very bored and begin to think of things to draw. Soon they are visualizing along with the class, and if they wait until it is time to draw rather than during the actual visualization exercise, I don't complain. The pictures are coming, vague at first, but with greater and greater clarity as we practice the different Journeys.

Making the Most of the Journey Elements

If you understand the reasons behind the basic elements of the Journeys in this manual, you will be able to use your decision-making skills to use, adapt, and perhaps create your own visualization exercises.

Scheduling

This section lets you know approximately how long each lesson will take, and how many exercises you need to do at different grade levels for optimal success of this program.

Purpose

From this information you can decide how many and which Journeys of each kind you will want to do.

Rationale

Studies tell us repeatedly that there is no particular program or strategy that works independently of the active and informed artistry and decision-making skills of the teachers who implement it. You are the element that makes the greatest difference in your classroom; the rationale sections are meant to give you the information that you need to make the best decisions for your students.

Preparation

This section will let you know what you need for each Journey.

Relaxation

A mind full of anticipation, worries, anger, or other tensions can easily interfere with concentration, causing students to miss a major part of each Journey because they are not in a relaxed state. There can also be some delightful side benefits to taking a moment to consciously relax before each Journey. Some studies suggest that when students relax before learning something new or before being tested, they learn, retain, and perform significantly better, so relaxation itself is a skill worth teaching (Osterroth 1993).

Visualization

Each exercise has been fully written out for you to read aloud. Use a calm voice and pause for about one second for each of the dots (. . . . . . .) that you encounter in the text.

If you decide to add some of your own visualization Journeys to your lesson plans, it is a mistake to think that you can create a mind's eye Journey on the spur of the moment. Visualization can be so powerful that it is vital that you write out a full script for each lesson and rehearse it, with the intent of eliciting pleasant and reassuring images. I suggest that you tape any new scripts that you create and then listen to them, putting yourself in your students' place, experiencing the timing and the content for yourself.

Grounding

Immediately after each visualization, students need to give a physical expression to their images or they will vanish, as does a dream before breakfast. While this grounding can be any kind of physical expression—writing, drawing, sculpting, singing, explaining, painting, and so on, drawing is easy and effective, especially in a classroom setting.

If some students worry about their drawing abilities, try these suggestions:

1. Explain regularly that their drawings are not supposed to be artistic, but just rough, quick sketches meant to help them remember their ideas.

2. You draw at the same time the students are drawing, and go out of your way to make your sketches very rough and nonartistic. (For me, this proved to be a natural talent, or lack thereof!)

3. Give students crayons, oil pastels, or broad-tipped felt markers rather than pencils and erasers which can lead to fussiness and attempts at perfection.

Sharing

After every Journey, offer students the opportunity to share their experience as suggested in each lesson plan. There are no right or wrong ways to visualize, so all answers are acceptable, and students should never be allowed to make fun of anyone's work. I often share my drawings both to be a part of the group experience and to model the lack of perfection in my drawings. After each child shares, it is fun to ask for a show of hands to see how many other students have visualized a similar thing.

Sharing has several important benefits:

1. It is enjoyable for students to see how their ideas are sometimes unique and sometimes shared by many others as part of the human family.

2. Students see a wide range of images and acceptable ways to represent those ideas by sketching.

3. As Joseph Campbell points out in *Hero with a Thousand Faces* (1949), there is an essential form and character to all great myths and journeys. In the final step of all journeys, the heroes return to share what they have learned or gained with the whole community. Only with this act of sharing does the journey complete its full meaning. Inasmuch as these students are each asked to create a unique image to learn or gain something of value, it is a fitting conclusion that they share their riches with their classmates. It brings an important sense of completion to the activity.

Evaluation

Process Evaluation

During the sensory exercises in Section I: Developing the Mind's Eye, the most important element to assess is how richly students are beginning to visualize. The goal of all of the activities in section I is to get all of your students making clear mental images. This is where your focus of evaluation should be. While they are working, you should circulate and ask questions about what students are drawing. If they are having difficulty visualizing, follow the suggestions found on page xv, under Important Hints to Optimize Success.

The other element to monitor is whether your students are enjoying and fully engaging in these exercises. Especially for your lower readers, these exercises are designed to involve students in a new approach to learning to read, and you should be looking for their full participation and intervening, if necessary, to increase students' participation.

In sections II and III you will be looking for evidence that students are still visualizing and that they are fully participating in each new activity.

Product Evaluation

Students' work products from learning the skills associated with visualization should be graded for participation only. This can be handled in several ways:

1. Have students keep their work in a visualization portfolio. This can be sent home at the end of the first four- to six-week program with a letter of explanation to parents about the exercise of mental muscles and the resulting increase in reading comprehension and writing fluency and creativity.

2. Assign each completed product a number of points toward the reading grade. All completed work gains full credit. Let students keep track of their point total, perhaps on the outside of their portfolios. After students are writing instead of drawing, you might choose to give points on the basis of quantity written (one point for an insufficient amount, two for the expected amount, and three for above and beyond).

3. Give a sticker or stamp that signifies "Full Credit" to each work.

Final Evaluation

Ultimately, you will evaluate the success of this program by your students' success in reading, which may be reflected in standardized tests or informal classroom measures, such as running records. Many teachers ask their reading specialists to pretest and posttest their lower readers before beginning the program and again after four or five months or at the end of the year. My own goals were for added enjoyment as well as added ability, so I also asked my students' parents whether their children were enjoying reading more than ever before, and I got a resounding yes from nearly all.

Section I

Developing the Mind's Eye

Before You Begin

For a new project to be successfully implemented, both teacher and students must be well prepared.

Prepare Yourself

Read through the manual and make a plan for implementing this program. Any of the exercises can be done at any time, but in order to be sure that you are helping all of your students to develop the skills of visualizing when they read, you should implement the series of lessons that are designed to kindle these skills. See How to Use This Manual on page xii to help you plan your approach.

Prepare Your Primary Students

Primary students are usually quite willing to shut their eyes and "see" images. Their experience will be enhanced if you explain that the mind's eye is like a muscle: To work at its best, the mind needs exercise in much the same way that the body does. Tell your students that over the next few weeks they will be doing "mind exercises." The exercises will be fun, but they will also be important schoolwork.

Prepare Your Intermediate or Upper-Grade Students

Your greatest task of preparation will be to convince your discouraged readers and writers to give this series of exercises a fair try. Children who have repeatedly failed at reading are likely to groan at yet another attempt to help them read. They have heard it all before, and nothing they have tried seemed to work.

Until these students are helped to understand that pictures created in their minds' eyes can help them make total sense of their daily reading, they will see no point in struggling once again with those printed words that have been dull, dry, and painful for them for so long. That is why I encourage the approach that begins with section I, so that these students will be caught off-guard by exercises that don't look anything like traditional reading and writing activities.

On the First Day with Intermediate or Upper-Grade Students

I start with a discussion of the human brain and how scientists are discovering that it can grow in power and strength every year of our lives. One of the ways we can help it grow and develop is through visualization. (Some teachers find that the words "internal television screen" or "mind movies" help children relate to this concept.) I explain how modern athletes, including Olympic hopefuls, have discovered that sometimes if they visualize a perfect game, their skills actually improve as much or more than if they had actually practiced (obviously within limits). This link with sports and exercise helps many students give these Journeys a try.

Next I engage the students in a very brief visualization exercise to demonstrate how painless and easy it can be. I say:

You are going to start by doing something you don't usually do in the classroom. You are going to close your eyes—and keep them closed while we all work through part of a lesson.

Shut your eyes just for the count of three. Ready, one, two, three. Great. Now for the count of five. One, two, three, four, five. Very good. Now close them just until you see the color red, then open them. (As eyes open, you can say, "I see Carli saw red, Tom did, and Marcy," etc.) Now shut your eyes long enough to see a pencil. It is a yellow school pencil. See if you can turn it red . . . . . (For each dot, leave about one second of silence.) How about purple, a purple pencil? . . . . .

Now open your eyes. Show me with your hands how long your pencil was. Raise your hand if it was sharp. Dull? Not sharpened at all? Raise your hand if you didn't see a pencil. That's fine, too. We are going to be learning how to make clearer and clearer mental pictures.

Using your mind's eye is just like using a muscle. The more you use it, the stronger it will become. If you do not see anything clearly yet, you can pretend that you see something. As you pretend, your visualization "muscle" will grow stronger.

Now you are ready to begin the first Journey. Proceed to section I, chapter 1.

1
Sensory Memories

Description

Students will be blindfolded and handed a sensory stimulus designed to elicit visual memories of similar sensations.

Scheduling

➤ **Now:** 30 minutes for five days to do all five exercises for all grade levels.

➤ **Later in the year:** You can return to the extension suggestions and create more of these Journeys any time you wish.

Purpose

These are essential exercises to take students from wherever they are in terms of levels of visualization and get them all visualizing at least to a minimal degree. The exercises use sensory stimulation to elicit pleasant personal memories—something that all children have stored somewhere in their brains—and turn those memories into visual images. Drawing is used to record these memories because we want to involve all children, even those who cannot read yet or discouraged readers turned off by requests for reading and writing.

Rationale

We must teach many students how to see a mental picture. It is a rare student who doesn't need at least some assistance in using the mind's eye when reading and writing; there is considerable evidence to suggest that poor readers are the very same students who cannot make a mental picture. Many teachers have discovered that teaching those poor readers how to form mental pictures can transform their reading, in terms of both comprehension and personal enjoyment.

We begin with sensory stimulation of early memories for several reasons. The first is that these exercises are fun and engaging. Students who have negative feelings about yet another attempt at learning reading skills readily become involved in this series of exercises with minimal resistance; before they know it they are visualizing and their reading is improving effortlessly.

Another reason to begin here is that studies on the body/brain connection reveal that our senses are often the quickest path to our memories. We have all experienced the flashback to childhood upon smelling a certain scent in the wind, a cookie in the oven, or Grandma's perfume. We can capitalize on this connection by giving children objects that will trigger pleasant memories. Then we can help them bring these memories into full awareness with vivid mental pictures.

Different children in your classroom may have different dominant senses. For one child hearing will elicit the strongest memories, for another smell, taste, or touch. Because of this, the exercises in this manual include all of the senses in each Journey, even if the connection seems far-fetched, as when we ask students to notice the color of sounds. The ability to cross over from one sense to another is essential in the understanding of metaphor in poetry and literature.

Marshmallow Journey

Materials Needed

For each student:

- Memory Book, below
- Crayons
- One large marshmallow
- Blindfold

For the teacher:

- Several extra marshmallows to replace those that are dropped or disappear in the dark.

Preparation

Note: It is essential to read through the material *before the lesson*, so you will know where the Journey is going.

- Do the preparation suggestions starting on page 1.

- For each student, create a Memory Book made of five sheets of white paper with two sheets of colored construction paper for the cover. Staple together along the edge. One page will be used in each of the following activities.

- Have students wash their hands.

Starting the Lesson

1. Ask your students if they can keep a secret. Tell them that you are going to hand them a surprise every day for the next week, if they can keep from telling anyone else what the object is until the lights are turned back on.

2. Distribute the Memory Books, crayons, and blindfolds. Have students put their names on the covers of the books. On the first white page, ask them to write the title, Memory Book. Then turn to the next page where they

will draw on both white pages later. Tell students to keep the books open to that spot and set their crayons aside in a place very easy to reach.

3. Tell your students that the purpose of this Journey is not to guess what you hand them, but to let the object help them see pictures and recall times when they have experienced similar objects. The more pictures or memories they can generate, the better.

4. Explain that their blindfolds will help them concentrate on their own mind pictures and remind them not to look to see what they are given. Tell them that their curiosity to see what you hand them would tempt them to open their eyes if they did not wear blindfolds.

5. Caution students not to take off their blindfolds in order to find objects they might drop. Keeping their blindfolds on, they should just raise their hands, and you will replace the object.

Relaxation

When the students take a minute to relax and prepare for the activity to come, they are ready to begin the exercise with you. Cares, worries, frustrations, or tension from the playground or from other schoolwork can be set aside in this brief exercise.

For this first relaxation exercise, I have included below the one that I do most frequently because it is brief and it involves all students quickly and effectively in physical movement. For all of the other Journeys in this manual, you can select any of a number of relaxation exercises included in the appendix, page 144.

In my kindergarten and first grades, I use the exercise offered on this page, Tense and Relax, to begin most of my journeys. I found that the predictability was in itself a relaxing agent. For older students, I started with Tense and Relax for several days and then went to Tension Dial, which I found to be a very powerful exercise for teaching students the ability to fully relax mind and body. I next began to try other options, as my students seemed to want some variety.

When you are ready to begin, dim the lights and leave them off. Tell students that when you do this each day it will be a signal to put their blindfolds on. Emphasize quiet, slow movements. Then read the relaxation exercise below:

Tense and Relax

Boys and girls, before we go on our Journey today, we are going to take just a moment to relax and get ready. Please sit up as comfortably and as straight as you can. . . . .Don't be stiff, just balanced and relaxed. Put your feet flat on the floor, and let your arms and hands be in the most relaxed and comfortable position that you can. . . . . Now slowly raise your hands above your head, and as you do, take in a slow, deep breath. . . . .Squeeze your hands into fists and squeeze and squeeze. . . . .and squeeze tighter. . . . .and then let your hands and arms relax and slowly let them go back down to your desk while you let out your breath and say, "AAAHHHH." Slowly, slowly. . . . .

Once more, raise your hands over your head and take a nice, slow, deep breath. Make fists again and squeeze. . . . .and squeeze. . . . .and then say, "AAAHHHH" and let your hands slowly come back down to rest on your desk or in your lap. Once more, raise your hands and squeeze with your fists. . . . .now add all the muscles in your arms and shoulders. . . . .squeeze and tighten all these muscles . . . .and then say, "AAAHHHH," and let your hands very slowly relax and come back down to rest comfortably. . . . .

Visualization

In just a minute I am going to hand something to you. Do not try to guess what it is; that is not important. If you do think of what the object is, please do not call out its name. I want everyone to get a chance to experience this object so that your mind's eye will remember other times you have felt something like this.

When I give you your object, please hold it quietly in your hands. It will take me a little while to get around the room. Do not do anything with the object until I tell you. Now put your hands out in front of you and hold them together so that I can drop something in them. If you drop this object, do not remove your blindfold and look for it. Just raise your hand, and I will give you another.

(Now hand out the marshmallows, going last to those students whom you suspect will have trouble keeping quiet about them.)

You probably all know what this might be, but now I want you to see what pictures you can get in your mind's eye. Not a picture of this object, but pictures or memories of other times you have felt this object in your hands. Now, keeping your mind's eye open to anything you might remember, please take the object in one hand and rub it on the back of your other hand very gently . . . . Now, tap it gently on your palm . . . . . When have you felt something like this? . . . . . Now change hands and do the same thing, first rubbing the back of your hand . . . . then tapping softly on the palm . . . . Keeping your mind's eye open to other times you have felt this sensation . . . . . Now hold the object in one hand and tap it softly on your cheek . . . . What color do you suppose this object is? . . . . Now hold the object with your other hand . . . Bring it up to one ear . . . . Lightly tap just the outside of your ear with the object and notice what sound it makes . . . . Where have you heard this sound before? . . . . Keep your mind's eye open to memories of other times you have heard this sound or felt this feeling against your ear . . . . Try the other ear . . . . Keep it just on the outside of your ear . . . You may be guessing what it is; please do not tell us . . . Try to remember a time when you have heard this sound before. Don't tell me out loud; just think of a time you felt something like this.

(If you think you can do so, pick up your own marshmallow and follow as many of your own directions as possible. This helps you time the pauses in between directions, and it gives you the mental images to draw your own picture in the Grounding activity. It means a little juggling, but it is worthwhile.)

Now I want you to bring this object close to your nose without touching your nose . . . . . and take a tiny, tiny sniff . . . . . Let your mind's eye see a picture of a time when you smelled this smell before . . . . . Remember what you saw then . . . . . Now take another, deeper smell, slowly . . . . . As the smell travels down your throat, notice the color of the smell . . . . Keep your mind's eye open for more pictures of times you have smelled this smell . . . . What does it remind you of? Now bring the object to your mouth. Don't put the object in your mouth, but gently lick it and try to remember when you have felt this feeling on your tongue before . . . . . What have you tasted before that tasted like this? . . . . or smelled like this? . . . . or felt like this? . . . . Lick the object again. What does it remind you of? . . . . . Where were you when you tasted it? . . . . .

Now bring the object even closer to your mouth and take a small bite if you wish . . . . . chew . . . . . and swallow . . . . . What color goes down your throat? . . . . . Did the smell get stronger? . . . . . Take another tiny bite . . . . Listen to the sound of your chewing and swallowing . . . . . What does this remind you of?

Grounding

Leave your blindfold on. Not yet, but in just a minute, I will ask you to take off your blindfold. When you do take it off, draw any pictures you saw with your mind's eye. Your pictures may show the colors you saw, or the memories you had.

Remember, I don't want you to draw just a picture of what this object is . . . . . I want to see memories and colors of what you saw with your mind's eye. No talking, please. Raise your hand quietly if you need help.

Ready, take off your blindfold, and finish eating the object if you wish or just set it on your desk. Then get your Memory Book and begin to draw. Draw as many different pictures as you can, pictures of things you remembered.

While the students are drawing, walk around and be sure they are on the right page of their books before you draw your own picture. Then circulate again. Quietly encourage the non-visualizers and non-drawers. Give them extra help if needed, as described on page xv, How to Use this Manual. Ask some of the more reluctant sharers to tell you a little about their pictures.

As some finish their drawings sooner than others, tell students that they are welcome to add words or sentences to their pictures if they wish. For primary students you might let them use phonetic spelling; you will not have time to get around and help everyone spell correctly.

Sharing

Ask for volunteers to tell about their pictures and their memories. Share your own picture to start things off. Point out to students that memories can be similar by asking questions like these: "How many saw a cup of hot chocolate, like Sam did?" or "Sue saw a kitten; did anyone else see that when they touched the marshmallow with their palm?"

Always remember that sharing must be voluntary because some memories may be personal.

Evaluation

In these first exercises, the only evaluation you need to do is to keep track of who is and who is not visualizing. If there are students who continue to have difficulty visualizing, you will need to work with them individually, using suggestions from page xv of How to Use this Manual.

Peanut Brittle Journey

Materials Needed

For each student:

- ✎ Memory Book, page 5
- ✎ Crayons
- ✎ Blindfold
- ✎ Piece of peanut brittle (a mint Lifesaver will also work)
- ✎ Moist paper towel for wiping up afterwards

Preparation

- Have students wash their hands.

- Screen students for possible peanut allergies and provide an alternative.

- Remind students that the purpose of the Journey is not to guess what you hand them, but to let the object help them see pictures and recall times when they have experienced similar objects. The more pictures they can generate, the better.

- Distribute Memory Books, crayons, blindfolds, and paper towels. Have students put books and crayons in an easily accessible place.

- Remind students that if they drop the object you will give them, they are not to take off their blindfolds and look for it, but raise their hands for assistance.

- Dim lights as a signal to put on blindfolds; leave lights off.

- Remind students that the first part of the Journey will be for relaxation, to clear their minds of outside thoughts or concerns and to help them focus on today's activity.

Relaxation

Do the same Tense and Relax exercise from the Marshmallow Journey, page 6.

Visualization

Today on our Journey, I am going to hand you something. Hold out both of your hands, and I will drop something in them. Remember, it is not important to guess what it is; you will be looking for memories of times when you felt something similar. If you happen to guess what the object is, please do not call out the name. I want everyone to have a chance to be surprised by it.

(Hand out a piece of peanut brittle or a mint Lifesaver to each student.)

As I hand you today's object, please hold it quietly until I give you instructions.

Hold the object in one hand, and gently tap it on your desk top . . . . . . Stop. . . . . Now listen for the color of the sound that it makes as you lightly begin tapping again . . . . Tap lightly, but quickly . . . . . Stop. . . . . Does this sound remind you of something?

Tap more slowly this time . . . . . . and stop. Now hold it in the palm of your other hand and tap it with the fingernails of your free hand . . . . . Keep your imagination open for any pictures that you are reminded of . . . . Now pinch it lightly and feel it with both hands . . . . . Turn the object around and explore it all over . . . . . What do you notice about its surface? . . . . . Have you felt something like this before?

Now bring the object up to one ear, and again tap it with your fingernails and listen to the sounds . . . . Now scratch on it . . . . What does this sound make you think of? . . . . . Now try the other ear, tapping it . . . . and scratching it . . . . Now hold it under your nose and smell . . . . When have you smelled something like this before? . . . . Now stick out your tongue and lick it . . . . . Notice the color of the taste as it touches your tongue . . . . . Lick it again, but don't put it inside your mouth just yet . . . . Now tap it softly against your top teeth . . . . . tap it gently against your bottom teeth . . . . . What other times have you heard this sound? . . . . .

Now, using your top and bottom teeth, bite off the tiniest piece that you can possibly manage . . . Hold that piece in your mouth until it melts . . . . . (If you do this too, you will have the best sense of the time it will take) . . . Now even if the tiny piece isn't melted, chew and swallow it . . . . Now, again paying attention to the sounds you make, bite off a little bigger piece and chew and swallow it as fast as you can . . . . Listen to the sounds . . . . . What do they remind you of? . . . . Notice the color of this taste as it goes down your throat . . . . Now you may eat the rest of this object if you like, quickly or slowly. I will give you one minute.

(After one minute has passed):

If you are not finished, you may either put the rest of the object in your mouth or in your desk. I don't want anyone to look at this object until we have finished our pictures, so please put it in your desk now.

Grounding

In just a minute, not yet, I will ask you to remove your blindfolds and draw any of the pictures that you saw. Your pictures can show the colors that you saw, or the memories that you had. They could even be pictures of designs or patterns that you made up. Remember, I am not asking for pictures of what you think the object was. I want pictures of things it reminded you of. If you have any questions, please raise your hand, and I will come to your desk. Do not talk or whisper. I want everyone to concentrate on the drawing until all work is finished. Ready, take off the blindfolds, wipe your hands, and begin to sketch.

While the students are drawing, make your own picture and then circulate. Quietly ask for some of the more reluctant sharers to tell you a little about their pictures, and encourage the non-visualizers and non-drawers. For students who finish their work quickly, you can offer the option of adding words or sentences to their sketches.

Sharing

Ask for volunteers to tell about their pictures and their memories. You might share yours. Let students notice where their pictures and memories are similar to their classmates. Remember, this is always a voluntary activity, as some visualizations may be very personal.

Evaluation

As before, page 9.

Ice Cube Journey

Materials Needed

For each student:

- Memory Book, page 5
- Crayons
- Blindfold
- Large ice cube or small, washed, and still wet smooth stones, about the size of a large marble or larger
- Moist paper towel for wiping up afterwards

For the teacher:

- Several extra ice cubes to replace those that are dropped or disappear in the dark

Preparation

- Remind students of the purpose of the Journey.

- Distribute Memory Books, crayons, blindfolds, and paper towels for the ice cubes. Have students put books, crayons, and paper towel on their desks.

- Remind students to raise their hands if they drop the object, and not to take off blindfolds and search for it.

- Have students take off jackets and sweaters, and roll up sleeves as far as possible.

- Dim lights as a signal to put on blindfolds; leave lights off.

Relaxation

Do the same Tense and Relax exercise from the Marshmallow Journey, page 6.

Visualization

Please turn in your seat now so that you can hold your hands out in front of you but not over your desk top. What I am going to hand you today could get your desk top messy, so I want your hands out in front of you, over the floor, not over your desk. Please keep your hands out together, and I will put something in them. Do not guess what this object is; just look in your mind's eye for any pictures that this object may remind you of. If you know what the object is, please do not call out its name. I want all students to get a chance to feel it themselves.

(Hand one large ice cube or stone to each student.)

Now hold this object in just one hand . . . . . rub it on the back of your other hand . . . . Now rub it on your arm, up and down . . . outside and inside . . . . . Change hands and just hold it quietly . . . Notice how it feels there in your hand . . . When have you felt this sensation before? . . . . (ice cubes only) Now with your mouth closed, put the object on your lips . . . . move it to a different part of the outside of your mouth . . . . . (ice cubes or stones) Now rub it on the back of your other hand . . . . Now on the other arm . . . up and down . . Now hold the object in both hands at once . . . . . Hold it in just one hand and touch it to your cheek . . . . the other cheek . . . .

(At this point, if you can do so, it is a good idea for you to pick up your own ice cube and follow your directions.)

Now hold the object in both hands and roll it around gently . . . . Have you ever felt something like this in your hands? Don't tell me out loud, but see the memory in your mind's eye . . . Where were you? . . . . .

(Compliment those who are following directions and not calling out.)

When have you felt a feeling like this before? . . . . . . Where were you? . . . . . . Who were you with? . . . . .

Now bring the object up to your neck, and softly rub the object along the front of your neck . . . . and very gently on the back of your neck . . . . .

(There will be giggles, but compliment the quiet ones.)

. . When have you felt something like this? . . . . Where were you? . . . What were you doing? . . . . . . Who were you with? . . . . . . Now put the surprise in your other hand and rub it on your chin . . . . and your cheeks . . . . . What does this remind you of?

Notice if you are reminded of memories of other times you have felt that sensation . . . . . Now smell it . . . . . What color does it smell like? . . . . . Touch this object to the tip of your nose . . . .

Now switch hands again, and touch the object to your knee if you can . . . . Put it at the back of your knee . . . . . Slide it down your leg . . . . . Notice if you are seeing other times when your leg felt like this . . . .

Now hold the object in both hands again, off to the side of your desk, and I will pick it up. Do not remove your blindfolds; I will show you what you have been holding after you have finished the pictures.

(Pick up the ice cubes.)

Grounding

Don't take off your blindfold yet, but when I tell you to take it off, you will draw some of the pictures that you saw. If you didn't see clear pictures, you can draw the colors or shapes that you saw. Raise your hand if you need help. Ready, take off the blindfold, use the paper towel to wipe up any water from your desk, and then begin to draw. No talking, please, so we can all remember and draw the pictures that we saw.

Once the children are drawing, you can quickly sketch your own memories and then circulate. If some students still aren't visualizing, continue to help them with suggestions found on page xv of How to Use This Manual.

As the quicker workers finish several sketches on the open page, tell the class that they can either continue to think of more to draw or label their drawings with words or sentences.

Sharing

Ask for a volunteer to tell one thing remembered. Have all children who shared that memory raise their hands. Continue in this fashion as long as there is interest. Students can hold up their drawings or not, as they wish.

Evaluation

As before, page 9.

Lemon Drop Journey

Materials Needed

For each student:

- Memory Book, page 5
- Crayons
- Blindfold
- Lemon drop or sprigs of pine needles, sage, or a cinnamon stick

Preparation

- Have students wash their hands.

- Remind students of the purpose of today's Journey: to open the mind's eye to memory pictures.

- Have students take off jackets and sweaters, and roll up sleeves.

- Remind them that if they drop the object, they should not remove blindfolds, but raise their hands, and you will assist them.

- Distribute Memory Books, crayons, and blindfolds.

- Dim lights as a signal to put on blindfolds; leave lights off.

Relaxation

For primary: Repeat the Tense and Relax exercise, page 6.

For intermediate and upper: Try a new exercise from the appendix, such as Tension Dial, page 145.

Visualization

Now, please put your hands together and hold them over your desk so that I can put something in them. When you get today's object, hold it quietly until I give you some instructions. Remember, it is not important to guess what the object is; it is your job today to see the memories the object brings to your mind's eye. Perhaps the object will smell like something you have smelled before. Maybe the sounds it makes will remind you of another place you have been, or of sounds you have heard somewhere else. If you guess what the object is, please do not call out its name. I want everyone to have the chance to encounter this object without any preconceived ideas.

If you drop the object on the floor, be sure to raise your hand and let me recover it. Do not remove your blindfold, or try to find the object yourself.

(Put a lemon drop in each student's hands, saving the last ones for students most likely to have trouble keeping quiet about the nature of the object.)

Now hold this object with the fingers of one hand and lightly brush it on the back of your other hand . . . . Now brush it on your palm and fingers . . . . Keep your mind's eye open for other times when you have felt this sensation . . . . Now brush your wrist . . . . and the inside of your arm . . . . . and the outside of your arm . . . . Hold the object with the fingers of the other hand . . . and again brush it lightly against the back of your empty hand . . . . . . and against your palm and fingers . . . . . . your wrist . . . . . . your inner arm . . . . . . your outer arm . . . . . .

Now, keeping the object in your hand, poke your arm and your empty hand with the end of this object . . . . See if you have felt this kind of a poke sometime before . . . . What color are the pokes? . . .

Now move this object to one ear, and make some kind of sound against your ear . . . keep it on the outside of your ear . . . . Notice if you have heard this sound somewhere before . . . . . . Now make a different kind of sound . . . . What does that remind you of? . . . . . . What color does the sound seem to be? . . . . Now try the other ear, making one kind of sound . . . listen carefully . . . . and make another kind of sound . . . What color is this sound? Is it a hot or a cold sound? . . . . . Now bring the object right under your nose and gently smell . . . . . . Let yourself remember any other times you have smelled this smell . . . . Now take an even deeper sniff . . . . . Pay attention to the color of the smell as it travels into your nose and down into your lungs . . . . Does it stay the same color all the way down, or does it change as it travels along? . . . .

(For the lemon drop only):

Now put out your tongue and slowly lick this object three times on one side . . . . Then bring it up to your nose and smell it again. Notice what is happening inside your mouth . . . . . and let your mind's eye remember a time when this has happened to you before . . . . . . Take one more deep sniff, remembering any times you have smelled this smell before . . . . (lemon drop only) Now, if you wish, put the object in your mouth without biting it. Roll it around inside your mouth . . . . . Does this remind you of another time when you tasted something like this? . . . . You may leave it in your mouth now, or you may chew it up if you wish . . . . . (all other objects) Put this object on your desk and I will collect it.

Grounding

Please keep your blindfold on until I ask you to remove it. I want you to use your energy to quickly represent what you have imagined. If you waste time, you could forget what you saw in your mind's eye, so please do not talk or whisper. Ready, take off the blindfolds and begin. Draw as many different pictures as you saw in your mind's eye.

As the students begin to draw, you can create your own picture, and then walk around, encouraging any who are not yet visualizing or drawing. Urge nonvisualizing students to draw something.

Sharing

Call for volunteers to explain and share their pictures. Also share yours. Continue to accept and praise all efforts. Notice similar pictures, and contrast colors and pictures.

Evaluation

As before, page 9. Notice who is freely visualizing and who still needs help.

Drum Journey

Materials Needed

For each student:

- ✎ Memory Book, page 5
- ✎ Crayons
- ✎ Blindfold

For the teacher:

- ✎ A drum that makes a strong, solid sound when struck
  (Any percussion instrument could work as well.)

Preparation

- Distribute Memory Books, crayons, and blindfolds. Have students turn to the first empty page in the book, and then set the materials aside but within easy reach.

- Thank students for keeping the secret a surprise in the last Journey, and encourage them to do the same again today.

- Tell them that today you will not be handing them anything, but they will be listening to a sound that you will make.

- Dim lights as a signal to put on blindfolds; leave lights off.

Relaxation

For primary: Repeat the relaxation exercise from the Marshmallow Journey, page 6.

For intermediate and upper: Repeat the exercise you used earlier in the Lemon Drop Journey, page 16.

Visualization

Today I am going to ask you to use your ears instead of your hands to create pictures in your mind's eye. Imagine that your ears have been gently washed and scrubbed cleaner than they have ever been, and that you hear so clearly that you can hear a pin drop across the room. Be very quiet today, so that everyone can hear the object, and if you think you know what it is, I'm sure you'll remember not to call it out.

You know by now that I don't want you to guess what this is that I am holding. I want you to let the sounds bring up pictures of other times you have heard these sounds.

Listen . . . . .(Strike the drum five or six times.) . . . . When have you heard this sound before? . . . . .(Do it again five times.) . . . . Were you outside? . . . or inside? . . . . . Were you hot or cold? . . . . Were you alone? . . . . . or with friends? . . . . . . What were you touching? . . . . (Strike the drum again five times.) . . . . . *How did you feel? . . .*

(Move to another part of the room.) *This time I want you to imagine that you can see the sound as it travels through the air to your ear. Let your mind's eye notice if it travels straight to your ear or zigzags or curves . . . . .*(Five more strikes, slower this time.) . . . . . *Again, watch how the sound travels with your mind's eye . . .*

(Five more strikes.) . . . *What color is this sound? . . . . .* (And five more strikes, faster now.) . . . . .

Listen once more to the sound and try to think of something else that this sound could be. . . (One strike.) . . . . *or what else?* (Three strikes, ... then five strikes in a different rhythm.)

Grounding

(Put the drum away so the students can't see it until after they draw.)

Ready, take off your blindfold and draw your pictures. Remember, don't just draw what you think I was holding, but draw what you remember doing with it or what someone else was doing. Or you may draw the pictures you saw of how the sounds traveled across the room to your ear. No talking, and raise your hand if you need help.

Draw and circulate. As some students finish, offer them the choice to label their pictures with words or sentences.

Sharing

Ask for volunteers to share. Share your picture. Discuss the idea of sounds having colors. Discuss the different ways the children saw sound move through the air. Let students hold up the pictures of how the sounds looked to them.

Evaluation

All students should be visualizing and drawing by now, at least to some extent. Collect Memory Books to give credit for participation.

Extended Activities for Sensory Memories

You may wish to do more than five Sensory Journeys with your students because the exercises are fun and because they are a very powerful way to increase visualization skills. If you have some students who are not responding as quickly as you would like after the initial five lessons, you may wish to create more Journeys right away. If everyone is visualizing consistently, you may wish to sprinkle this type of activity into your program throughout the year, as a treat.

Here are some ideas to help you with further Sensory Journeys:

Sensory Journeys Involving Taste

Using the general format of the Peanut Brittle Journey, page 10, find a food that you think will elicit early memories in your own students. A square of chocolate, a candy cane, a caramel, a stick of gum, a Hershey's kiss, an orange slice, and a mint Lifesaver are some ideas to get you started thinking.

Sensory Journeys Involving Touch

Using the general format of the Ice Cube Journey, page 13, find items that your students would associate with happy memories. You might consider a bit of satin, a stuffed animal, acorns or leaves from the trees where you live, and modeling clay.

Sensory Journeys Involving Hearing

Using the general format of the Drum Journey, page 19, pick an object you can hold and make sounds with, as in that Journey. Or you can choose to give each student something with which to make noise. If students hold their own noise-makers, you will have to alter the basic script to a greater extent.

Some objects students might hold to make sounds: party noisemakers, pipes, children's toys that make a sound, song flutes, Halloween clickers, poker chips, beans in a paper cup, or a handful of wrinkled tissue paper or newspaper.

Some objects that you might use to make sounds: a timpani, a flute, a piano, good tones from any instrument you can play (violin, tuba, clarinet, etc.), an electric mixer, an alarm clock bell, a xylophone, a bouncing ball, or a gong.

Sensory Journeys Involving Smell

Using the general format of the Lemon Drop Journey, page 16, substitute any smell that would be very familiar to your children. Baby powder sprinkled on a cotton ball stimulates many memories. Fragrant flowers or leaves that most children experience or common spices from the cupboard will also work. (Be careful with fresh bay laurel or eucalyptus leaves; their scent can be overwhelming and the leaves can be sharp when crushed.)

General Guidelines

- Unless you simply alter and use the scripts that I have provided for you, be sure to prepare your extended activity lesson by writing out any script you create for your class. It is a mistake to think that you can make up a script as you go along.

- After you write your own script, read it into a tape recorder, and then listen to it as you follow the directions. In this way you will discover any potential problems before your class does.

- Before each Sensory Journey begins, use one of the relaxation exercises from this manual, or perhaps one that you discover elsewhere. If you skip the relaxation, many students do not tune in for the first part of the lesson.

2

Best Memories—In the Corners of Your Mind

Description

Blindfolded students will be asked to remember a pleasant early memory and recall the senses associated with it.

Scheduling

➤ **Now:** 20–30 minutes for two days for all grade levels to do Best Fireworks, page 25, and Best Water Fun, page 30.

➤ **Later in the year:** Do the other two exercises and develop more extensions if you wish.

Purpose

The next step in developing vivid imaging is to ask students to recall pleasant memories from verbal cues, without any sensory stimulation at all.

Rationale

When we ask students to remember early times, we are developing their ability to see mind's eye images whenever they wish. This takes us a step closer to the kind of visualization required in reading and writing.

There is evidence, too, that as we provide the opportunity for students to remember early times, their memories become stronger and more reliable in present time, and we are actually improving the functioning of the mind.

Best Fireworks Journey

Materials Needed

For each student:

- ✎ Memory Book, page 5
- ✎ Crayons or oil pastels
- ✎ Blindfold

For the teacher:

- ✎ Optional: Tape or CD of soft, slow classical music

Preparation

- Make a Memory Book for each student using the directions on page 5.

- Tell students that the purpose of this exercise is to help them see pictures with their minds' eyes. Explain that their brain is like a muscle: the more they exercise it, the better it works.

- Distribute Memory Books. Have students write their name on the cover of the books, and the title, Memory Book, on the first white page. Then tell them to turn to the next page, where they will draw later.

- Distribute crayons and blindfolds. Have students turn to the next page in their books and then set them aside.

- Dim lights as a signal to put on blindfolds; leave lights off.

Relaxation

You might like to try a new relaxation exercise from the appendix, page 144, for this group of Journeys. You may opt to play some soft, slow classical music while you read the following:

Visualization

Today I want you to go back to a time when you saw some wonderful fireworks. Perhaps you saw a show on the Fourth of July, or you might even have seen a fireworks display on television.

Imagine now that it is getting dark and almost time for the fireworks. Try to recall how you felt when you were waiting for the fireworks to begin . . . . . Were you excited? . . . . . happy? . . . . . eager for the show to begin? . . . . . Remember how you felt as you waited for the fireworks to start.

What sounds did you hear as the fireworks started? . . . . . Were there booming sounds? . . . . . or hissing sounds? . . . . or whistling sounds? . . . . How did the sounds make you feel? . . . . . . Were there other sounds from the people you were with . . . . . laughing . . . . . or shouting . . . . . or running sounds . . . . . . clapping . . . . . . or talking . . . . . . or asking for more? . . . . . .

What smells did you smell as the fireworks went off? . . . . Was there a smoky smell? . . . . . Can you remember which had the strongest smell? . . . . Was there a smell of matches? . . . . . . Was there a smell from sparklers? . . . . . .

Look around on the ground . . . . is it grass, or concrete, or dirt? . . . . Were there any smaller fireworks that people were setting off? . . . . Watch and listen . . . . .

Can you remember the food that you ate that night? . . . . Did you have hot dogs? . . . . or popcorn? . . . . . What did you have to drink? . . . . . Can you taste it now? . . . . .

And now let yourself see the fireworks again, as clearly as if they were really here . . . . See your favorite go off . . . . . What colors do you see? . . . . See a different kind go off now. . . . . . . What color is it? Do you see more than one color in any of the fireworks? . . . . Do you see stars? . . . . . Remember how you felt as you watched all the colors of light.

Grounding

Now pay attention again to this room. In a minute you will take off your blindfold and draw. No talking, please. Raise your hand if you need me. Ready, go.

Circulate to collect blindfolds and be sure that each child is drawing something.

For primary:

When a few students have finished drawing, tell everyone to add the title "My Best Fireworks Memory." Spell the title for them if they need help. Then tell your class that they can also label their memory pictures with words or sentences. If they are unable to spell some of the words they need, suggest that they use invented spelling and write the words as they sound.

For upper grades:

Suggest that if they wish they can add a title and any description they want to write. Have a class discussion about what everyone recalled. Share your own fireworks memories with your class.

Sharing

As usual, page 12.

Evaluation

As in chapter 1, page 9, your primary focus will be to assess and support students' visualization skill development.

When the Memory Book is done, you can give the student participation credit.

Lost Tooth Journey

Materials Needed

For each student:

- Memory Book, page 5
- Crayons or oil pastels
- Blindfold

For the teacher:

- Optional: Tape or CD of soft, slow classical music

Preparation

- Be sure that each student in your class has lost a tooth. Skip this activity if your whole class cannot be a part of it.

- Remind students of the purpose of the activity.

- Distribute materials.

- Dim lights as a signal to put on blindfolds; leave lights off.

Relaxation

Use the suggestions on page 32.

Visualization

Now I want you to go back in time to when you first noticed a loose tooth in your mouth . . . . . Remember how it felt to touch that tooth with your tongue? . . . . . Can you remember how the tooth wiggled, just a little at first, and then a lot? . . . . . Let your tongue remember . . . . . How did you feel when you chewed on something when your tooth was loose?

Remember the noise that the tooth made when it moved? . . . . Did it click against the other teeth? . . . . or did it sound squishy? . . . . . Let your ears remember . . . .

Now see the tooth when it came out of your mouth. Can you remember what it looked like? . . . . Remember what the tooth felt like when you touched it with your fingers . . . . . Where did you put it when it came out? . . . . . Who did you show it to? . . . . .

Now remember when you looked in the mirror . . . . . Did you stick your tongue in between your teeth, into that space where the tooth was . . . . Remember what it felt like to touch that space with your tongue . . . . .

Where is that tooth now? . . . .

Grounding

Now pay attention again to this room. When I tell you to take off your blindfold, draw pictures that you remember from the time you lost that tooth. Don't talk, please. If you need me, raise your hand. Ready. Take off your blindfold and draw.

Circulate as usual, draw a picture, and then talk to students as they work. As some students finish, give a title for the page: My Lost Tooth. Then suggest that students add captions to their sketches, if they have time.

Sharing

As usual, page 12.

Evaluation

As before, page 9.

Best Water Fun Journey

Materials Needed

For each student:

- ✎ Memory Book, page 5
- ✎ Crayons or oil pastels
- ✎ Blindfold

For the teacher:

- ✎ Optional: Tape or CD of soft, slow classical music

Preparation

- Remind students of the purpose of the exercise.

- Distribute Memory Books, crayons, and blindfolds. Have students open their books to the next page and set the book aside.

- Dim lights as a signal to put on blindfolds; leave lights off.

Relaxation

Use the suggestions on page 32.

Visualization

(Blindfolds should be in place.)

Today you are going back to a warm summer day when you were very young, and the grownups let you play in some water. Maybe you got to play with a hose . . . . Maybe you played in the sprinkler . . . . Maybe it was a Slip-and-Slide . . . . . Or was it a little pool out in the backyard?

Imagine that the day is warm, the sun is shining, and you are playing with the water. Notice what you are wearing . . . . . Notice how warm or cool you feel . . .

. . . What are your feet touching? . . . . Are you barefoot, or do you have shoes that you are getting wet? . . .

When you sit down, or maybe fall down, what do you feel then? . . . . . Is it grass? . . . . or water? . . . . . . or dirt? . . . . . or something slippery? . . . . . Can you feel the air on your body . . . . . or on your wet clothes? . . . .

Now notice what sounds the water is making . . . . . Just listen . . . . . . Can you hear any other sounds as you play in the water? . . . . Are any friends with you, talking or laughing? . . . . . Can you hear the grownups' voices, or is it quiet except for the water sounds? . . . .

Can you taste the water? . . . . Does it slide down your face and slip into your mouth? . . . .

Now look around and see what you can see . . . . . What is on the ground? . . . . What color is it? . . . . . Where are you? . . . . . In your own yard . . . . . or someone else's? . . . .

Now look at the water you are playing with . . . . . . What color is it? . . . . Where is it coming from? . . . . . What does it look like when you touch it? . . . when you splash it? . .

Grounding

Now pay attention again to this room. In just a minute you will take off your blindfold and draw at least one of the pictures you saw. No talking, please. Just raise your hand if you need help. Ready, take off your blindfold and begin to draw.

Circulate, talk to students, and give encouragement as you move around. When you can, draw your own brief sketch. Then, when a few students have finished drawing, suggest a title for all to write on their page: Water Fun. Next, tell students to label their individual pictures with words or sentences.

Sharing

As usual, page 12.

Evaluation

As before, page 9.

Best Birthday Journey

Materials Needed

For each student:

- ✎ Memory Book, page 5
- ✎ Crayons or oil pastels
- ✎ Blindfold

For the teacher:

- ✎ Optional: Tape or CD of soft, slow classical music

Preparation

- Remind students of the purpose of the Journey

- Distribute the Memory Books, crayons, and blindfolds.

- Dim lights as a signal to put on blindfolds; leave lights off.

Relaxation

Use the same relaxation exercise you chose for the Best Fireworks Journey, page 25, or any other from the appendix, page 144. Play soft music if you wish.

Visualization

Today I want you to go back to the very best birthday party you ever attended when you were younger. It might have been your own . . . . . or it might have been a friend's . . . . . or a cousin's . . . . If you don't attend birthday parties, it could be any party that you have ever enjoyed . . . . See if you can go back to it now and enjoy it all over again.

First remember the tastes at the party . . . . . Was there something good to eat? . . . . . Imagine that you are tasting again . . . . chewing . . . . . enjoying . . . . . . swallowing . . . . . Was there something else to eat? . . . Something cold, or something warm? . . . . . . Imagine that you are eating it now . . . . . Was there something to drink? . . . . . . Without making any noise, imagine that you are drinking it now.

Now let's remember sounds at the best party . . . . . Listen for any happy sounds that you heard there . . . . . . Are there any friendly voices? . . . . . What are they saying? . . . . . or singing? . . . . Are there other sounds? . . . . Any popping sounds? . . . . or tearing sounds as presents are opened? . . . . any laughing sounds? . . . . . .

And what do you remember seeing? . . . . Friends' faces . . . . Presents waiting to be opened . . . . . . What color are they? . . . . Do you see a birthday cake, or cupcakes? . . . . . ice cream? . . . . . or cookies? . . . . . or candy? . . . . . . How about balloons? . . . Where are they? . . . . . . What color are they? . . . . . Look around and see where the party is . . . . . Inside or outside? . . . . . What is all around you? . . . . .

Now let your hands remember anything you touched at this party? . . . . . Were you opening presents? . . . . How did that feel? . . . . Did you play any games? . . . . . What were you holding while you played the games? . . . . . Can you feel it now? . . . . Did your hands get sticky when you ate the treats? . . . . .

Grounding

Now pay attention again to this room.

Get ready, and when I say "go," take off your blindfold and begin drawing what you saw in your mind's eye. Ready, go. Draw as many pictures as you have time for on the page we opened in our books.

Circulate as usual, talking about what the students are drawing, then quickly sketch your own memories. As some students finish, suggest a title: My Best Birthday Memory. Then tell students to write captions near their pictures. Continue to help students who need extra help with visualizing.

Sharing

As usual, page 12.

Evaluation

As before, page 9.

Extended Activities for Best Memories

Here are some ideas for creating other Memory Journeys. Remember to keep the memories positive. For maximum effectiveness, write your own visualizations out in full script form, and practice with the tape recorder before working with your class.

Remember to talk about all five senses in each exercise: touch, taste, smell, sight, and hearing. Some children's memories will be triggered more easily by different senses.

These ideas will work for K–3 students. Some older students may think them too childish if done with the whole class, but when done as part of a pull-out program they could work, depending on the child.

Early happy memories
First pet
First secret hiding place
First good friend
First favorite toy
First stuffed animal
First time you helped cook
First Halloween costume
First playground
First tricycle or Kiddie Car
First bed

3

Listen My Children and You Shall See

Description

Blindfolded, students are to image familiar objects (trees, shapes, animals), and then to change their color, size, or position in space.

Scheduling

➤ **Now:** 30–40 minutes for two or three days to do either any two or all three exercises at all grade levels.

➤ **Later in the year:** You can do the third exercise, or develop any of the Extensions if you wish.

Purpose

Next we want students to be able to see an image that comes from the textual input, rather than just from personal memories.

Rationale

The skill that we develop here, that of imaging objects and action, is an essential part of making reading come to life in the mind's eye. The printed page says much, but it does not specifically direct the reader to visualize it. Many students have not imaged as they read. We begin to change that by purposefully showing them how to create moving pictures and to alter them at will.

Ice-Cream Cone Journey

Materials Needed

For each student:

- ✎ Art paper
- ✎ Crayons or pastels
- ✎ Blindfold

Preparation

- Distribute materials and blindfolds.

- It is important to remind students that you want them to create pictures in their mind's eye and that they will be drawing what they see.

- Dim lights as a signal to put on blindfolds; leave lights off.

Relaxation

You can select any relaxation exercise from the appendix, page 144, either a familiar one or something new for this set of exercises.

Visualization

Today in your mind's eye I want you to picture an empty ice-cream cone . . . . . no ice cream in it yet, just empty . . . . . What shape is the ice-cream cone? . . . . . Notice what color it is . . . . . Now make it green . . . . . . See if you can turn it blue . . . . . .Now make it be a regular cone color . . . . . Turn it upside down . . . . . then sideways . . . . . then right side up. Now make it pointed at the bottom . . . . . . Now make it flat on the bottom . . . . . . Now make it into your favorite kind of empty ice-cream cone.

It is time to add the ice cream. First, add a scoop of chocolate . . . . . . Then, make the chocolate disappear and put in a scoop of vanilla . . . . . . Now the vanilla disappears, and instead you see a scoop of strawberry . . . . . . Now make the strawberry disappear and put a scoop of your favorite flavor into the ice-cream cone.

Leave your favorite flavor in the cone and, on top of it, put a scoop of chocolate . . . . . Now there are two scoops: your favorite on the bottom . . . and chocolate on the top. Add another scoop on top of the chocolate . . . . Now there are three scoops . . . . . What color is the third scoop? . . . . Now add another scoop . . . and another . . . . and another . . . . keep adding until the cone is as tall as a house . . . . .

Now imagine that all the ice cream in the cone turns into snowflakes. . . . . . snowflakes in all of the colors of the ice cream. . . . .and a gentle breeze blows them up into the bright blue sky and over the tops of the houses. . . . . .and the ice-cream cone is empty once more. . . . .

Now start to fill the cone with your absolute favorite flavors. First, put on one scoop of a flavor of ice cream that you really love to eat. Then look at this ice-cream cone and decide if it is just right for you as it is, or if you would like to add some more ice cream. . . . . Maybe you would like to add another scoop of the same flavor, or maybe you would like to add a different favorite flavor. . . . . Take your time, and put exactly the flavors that you would want in your perfect ice-cream cone. . . . . .Then you can image eating it all up. . . . .

Now bring your attention back to the classroom. Feel your feet on the floor and notice the sounds around you.

Grounding

When I ask you to take off your blindfold, you will draw your favorite ice cream image. Label the different flavors. Remember, do not talk, but go right to work. Raise your hand if you need help. Ready, begin.

Sharing

Students can tell about their pictures. For primary grades, you could collect and bind everyone's pictures together into a class book each day. (These pictures are seldom so personal that they cannot be shared, as you are giving direct instructions about what to see.)

Evaluation

Continue to notice which students need extra help and encouragement. Always let students know that you value the quality of their efforts by your comments and by doing something special with the drawings. You might wish to store individual visualization portfolios where students keep all associated artwork.

Car Journey

Materials Needed

For each student:

 Art paper

Crayons or pastels

Blindfold

Preparation

- Distribute materials and blindfolds.

- It is important to remind students to watch their mind's eye movie screens.

- Dim lights as a signal to put on blindfolds; leave lights off.

Relaxation

Use the same relaxation exercises for all the Listen and See Journeys, page 144.

Visualization

Today, in your mind's eye, I would like you to picture a car. Any car at all . . . . . It could be your own family's car or one that you would like to have. It can be any car at all. Now turn this car red . . . . . . Can you turn the car yellow? . . . . . Now make it purple . . . . . . Now black . . . a black car . . . . . Now make it green with a white top . . . . Now turn the car any color you like best. If you want, you can add stripes . . . or any other design.

Now put the car on a dirt road in the country and watch your car move along. . . . . . Now see it on a four-lane highway . . . . Now on a twisting, turning road through a forest . . . . . . Now your car is moving along a road by the edge of the ocean . . . . . . Now, put it on the kind of road that you like best . . .

Take a good look at your car . . . . how many doors does it have? . . . . How many tires? . . . . . How many windows? . . . . . . .Let's change some things . . . . .

Make it longer . . . with two more doors for people to open . . . . . Make it even longer and give it two more doors . . . . . . Now make it the same as it was before . . . . Now make it taller . . . . As tall as a bus . . . . . . Then make it shorter again . . . . . Now give it wings, like an airplane, and let it take off into the sky . . . . . . Watch it fly through the sky . . . . Then let it land near a lake . . . . . .

Let it turn into a boat . . . and go sailing off onto the lake . . . . Watch it return to the shore, and as it comes out of the lake, it turns back into a car again . . . . . Now the car gets smaller . . . . and smaller . . . until it is a toy car that you can pick up and play with whenever you want.

Now feel the floor and your chair under you . . . . and notice the sounds in the room . . . .

Grounding

In just a minute, you will remove your blindfold and draw your favorite image. I know you saw lots of pictures; just draw the one that was the funniest or most interesting in some way. Don't forget to use the colors you saw with your mind's eye. Do not worry if you can't make your sketch look as great as what you saw in your mind's eye; our sketches are just meant to help us remember the vivid pictures of our imagination. Do not talk. If you need help, raise your hand, and I will come to your desk. Ready, begin.

Students who finish quickly can turn their papers over and draw another picture from their mind's eye Journey. They might like to give their cars a name, or label any special features.

Sharing

Volunteers can tell about their cars. You could put volunteers' work up for display, or in primary you could make individual or class books.

Evaluation

As before, page 37.

Apple Tree Journey

Materials Needed

For each student:

- ✎ Art paper
- ✎ Crayons
- ✎ Blindfold

Preparation

- Remind students that they will be seeing action as you talk, just as if there were a movie screen in their minds' eyes.

- Distribute paper, crayons, and blindfolds.

- Dim lights as a signal to put on blindfolds; leave lights off.

Relaxation

Use the same relaxation exercise for all the Listen and See Journeys, page 144.

Visualization

On our Journey today you find yourself in the middle of a large field where things can grow . . . . . In front of you is a freshly dug piece of rich earth . . . In your hand is a seed . . . It is an apple seed . . . You put the apple seed in the ground and water it . . . . . You can see it begin to grow . . . . . It is obviously a magic seed and will take just a minute to become a full-sized tree. Right now, watch it grow taller and taller . . . . . putting out more and more branches . . . . . Watch the leaves appear on those branches . . . Now the tree is taller than you are . . . Now it is as tall as your house . . . Now it is even taller . . . . Now blossoms start to appear all over the apple tree . . . hundreds and hundreds of blossoms . . . A gentle breeze comes along and the blossoms begin to float down from the tree and lie on the ground . . . . Where the blossoms were attached, you can see the tiny apples beginning to grow . . . They are green and very small . . . . . As you watch, they begin to grow larger and larger until they are as large as the apples you buy at the store . . . . Then they start to change color . . . first from green to yellow . . . then red streaks appear . . . and finally they are red all over . . . Look at this big green tree with hundreds and hundreds of round, ripe, red apples hanging from its branches . . . . .

Now, one at a time, not all at once, each apple turns into an orange . . . pop, pop, pop, pop, until every apple has become a fat, round, orange . . . . Now let each orange, one by one, turn into a banana. Pop, pop, pop, pop . . . . . Nothing but bananas now . . . Step back and see this big green apple tree covered with bananas. Yellow bananas hanging from every branch. Now, all at once, the bananas turn into skateboards . . . . . Hundreds and hundreds of skateboards hanging from a skateboard tree . . . . . Notice the colors and sizes of the skateboards . . . . . Now half of the skateboards turn into baseballs, and the other half become baseball bats . . . . .

Now the baseballs and baseball bats turn into stars and moons . . . . stars and moons hanging from the big green tree . . . shining . . . . . Let the stars and moons become forks and spoons . . . . . silver forks and spoons hanging from the branches . . . Now let all the forks and spoons turn into big yellow roses . . . . . Let the roses turn red . . . . . Let the red roses turn back into apples.

Now let's stand back and watch the red apples changing colors. First they all turn yellow . . . then all of them are sky blue . . . . . Now let's make the apples in the top half of the tree turn white, and the bottom half can turn pink . . . . . Now turn the apples at the bottom violet, and the apples at the top, silver . . . . . Next, let's turn all the green leaves to silver and the apples to gold . . . . . Now let's turn the leaves to red and the apples to green . . . . Now let's turn the leaves back to their usual green, but let the apples turn every color of the rainbow . . . .

Now let the apples stay all the different colors of the rainbow, but make them grow larger and larger until they begin to look more like balloons than apples . . . . . Balloons of every color . . . . . They are balloons, and as you watch, they begin to leave from the branches of the tree and slowly float upwards . . . . . All the balloons of every color are now floating gently up to the sky . . . . . You watch them as they grow smaller and smaller . . . . Look back at the apple tree, standing there very proud of all the images it was able to present to you . . . . And now please come back to this classroom. Feel the floor under your feet and the chair that is holding you up. Do not remove your blindfolds.

Grounding

Not yet, but in just a minute, I will ask you to take off your blindfolds and draw. Today I'd like you to draw the apple tree in one of its many changes. Choose one that you saw clearly or one that you particularly liked. If you have extra time, you can use the back of the paper to represent something else from this exercise. If you have any questions, please raise you hand, and I will come over to your desk. Do not talk, please. Ready, begin.

During the drawing, draw your picture and then circulate.

Sharing

As usual, ask for volunteers to tell about their pictures and show them, if they wish. This exercise usually results in some lovely pictures that are shown with pride. They make an attractive bulletin board.

Evaluation

As before, page 37.

Extended Activities for Listen and See Journeys

Here are some ideas for developing further Journeys similar to those provided in this chapter. They need not be a part of the basic program, but can provide further visualization experience now or later in the school year.

Use the following guidelines to help you plan your Journeys:

- Write out new scripts, drawing from the suggestions listed below.

- Experiment with programming or mind-mapping to help you plan your scripts.

- Try taping your script. Then, while listening to it, check your timing and correct mistakes.

- If you have a listening center and headphones, you could let students listen to your tapes individually in their free time.

Listen-and-See Journeys about Shapes

Create colored shapes—triangles, rectangles, circles, squares. Start with one and change its color, then its shape. Later put one shape inside another, or beside another and experiment with their colors. Let them bounce, grow or shrink, or move around. Make a shape turn into something appropriate, like turning a triangle and a circle into an ice cream cone, or turning a square and a triangle into a house with a steep roof.

Listen-and-See Journeys about Students' Homes

Tell students to visualize a visit to their own homes, changing the color of the walls, the rugs, the furniture. Have them move the furniture from one room to another and see how it looks. Put the furniture on the ceiling, put pictures on the floor. Have the popcorn popper malfunction and fill the house with popcorn up to their knees. Have the whole class come over to eat it.

Listen-and-See Journeys about Students' Own Backyards

Direct the students into their own backyards. Change the size and shape. Change the weather. Change the color of the grass, trees, or flowers. Put in different kinds of fences, different trees, waterfalls, rocks. Now tell students to change their yards to their idea of the perfect yard. Put in equipment, a swimming pool, a tetherball, a soccer field, a pet elephant, anything they might want. Next have them bring in people to share their new yard. Imagine children, adults, and animals.

Listen-and-See the Zoo

Direct the students to picture going to the zoo. Turn the animals different colors. Have them stand on their hind legs, their front legs, or balance on one leg. Watch them eat. Give them better cages, adding trees, swimming pools, and other comforts.

Touchy-Feelie Journey

Do not use blindfolds. Ask students to fold their paper into fourths. Ask them to put out their hands and imagine that there is something in them; the first time, have it be something sticky. Tell them to imagine how it feels, how it looks, and smells, how heavy or light it is. Then let them open their eyes and draw the image in one of the segments of their art paper. They can add any words for a label or description. Repeat this process with something smooth. Next time have them imagine that they are holding something bumpy. The next time, something cold. After each experience, have students draw what they saw on a section of their art paper.

4
Archetypes

Description

Blindfolded, students will be asked to image a common archetype (wicked witch, handsome prince). Students will then direct these archetypes to take action.

Scheduling

➤ **Now:** 40 minutes for two days for older students. For primary, go to section II.

➤ **Later in the year:** These two exercises, shortened to 20–30 minutes as indicated in the instructions, can be done at any time in the year for primary also.

Purpose

These exercises get students specifically imaging characters to prepare them for the characters they encounter in literature.

Rationale

Webster's Dictionary defines an archetype as: "the original model, form, or pattern from which something is made or from which something is developed."

Because each of us comes equipped with a set of archetypes, we can use those ready-made images as a first step in developing the skill of visualizing characters. For instance, we have a vivid notion of "wicked witch-ness". When we read or hear of a character, we compare it with our idea or archetype. We immediately know whether we are confronting a wicked witch or not, regardless of the description of clothing and appearance given by the writer. This is not a real witch, but an archetype that stretches across human cultures.

To fully appreciate a story, it is usually very important to be able to get a solid sense of the main characters, their strengths, weaknesses, needs, and desires. By beginning with archetypes whose characteristics are well known and widely agreed upon, students practice bringing storybook characters to life.

In this section, we begin the transition to using writing instead of drawing, to describe the visions of the mind's eye.

Archetypes on Parade

Materials Needed

For each student:

- ✎ Art paper
- ✎ Crayons
- ✎ Pencils
- ✎ Blindfold

For the teacher:

- ✎ A chart with the names of the following archetypes written in large letters: Beautiful Princess, Wicked Witch, Kindly Old King, Wizard, Good Fairy, Big Bad Wolf, Handsome Prince, Superhero

Preparation

- Tell your students that they are going to experience a new kind of Journey, one on which they will learn more characterization.

- Distribute the materials. Have students fold their paper into fourths and then open it again, providing four squares on the front and four on the back. Primary students will use front only.

- Dim the lights as a signal to put on blindfolds, or from this point on, students could be given the option to just shut their eyes.

Relaxation

Do this relaxation exercise because it leads into the Journey.

Please put your feet flat on the floor and begin to relax and center yourself . . . . Move your shoulders and arms and hands around as you like, and then put them on your desk top . . . . Take a few deep breaths, all the way in, letting the oxygen travel all the way down into your lungs and stomach . . . and all the way out . . . . . And again all the way in, this time letting the air go into your legs and all the way down to your feet and toes . . . And all the way out . . . .

We are going to begin today by going to a place where you love to be alone . . . . A place where you always feel safe and good . . . . . It could be outdoors . . . or indoors . . . It might be in your own house, or in someone else's . . . . . It might even be a place that you have read about or imagined . . . . Think of this place where you feel relaxed and safe and very good . . . . . And wherever it is, go there right now in your imagination. Feel yourself being there . . . . Notice the things you see there . . . . Look to the left . . . . . and to the right . . . . Look up and notice what you see . . . . and look down . . . . Now pay attention to the sounds in this place . . . . . .This is your own place . . . .

You can improve this place in any way you like . . . You can add improvements like furniture . . . . or buildings . . . . . or more warmth or coolness . . . . Whatever you like and whatever you need . . . . . And now I will be quiet for a moment while you just enjoy being in this place of your own . . . .

Now, wherever you are, I would like you to notice that there is a stage over to one side . . . . Notice its color and size . . . . The curtains are closed . . . . Very soon some characters are going to come out on this stage . . . . Let the lights in the room or in the sky begin to grow dim, so that you can easily see the stage, and you notice that the stage lights are starting to come on . . . . Get comfortable so that you can watch the show . . . The curtains are about to part . . . .

Visualization

As the curtains pull back, you see a Beautiful Princess in the middle of the stage . . . . Notice the color she is wearing . . . . Does she wear anything on her head? . . . . Is she holding anything? . . . . Do you hear any sounds? . . . . Watch to see what she is doing . . .

Now the Beautiful Princess disappears, and in her place you see a Wicked Witch . . . . Notice what she is wearing . . . . Notice how she walks . . . . Is she carrying anything? . . . . Listen to any noises you hear . . . . . See what she is doing . . . .

(For primary students only, continue with the following):

Now the Wicked Witch disappears, and in her place you see a Handsome Prince . . . . . Is he standing or sitting? What is he standing or sitting on? . . . . . Is he tall or short? . . . . . Is he dark or fair? . . . . . What is he wearing? . . . . . If he were looking for something, what do you think that might be? . . . . .

(For primary, skip to "For All Students," below)

(For intermediate students only, continue with the following):

Now the Wicked Witch disappears, and in her place you see a Kindly Old King . . . . . Is he standing or sitting? . . . . . What is he wearing? . . . . . Notice the color . . . . . Take a look and see what he is doing . . . . .

The Kindly Old King disappears . . in his place you see a Wizard . . . . . Notice what the Wizard is wearing . . . . . what he might be holding . . . . . Notice his size . . . . . And see the color of his clothing . . . . . Does he have anything on his head? . . . . . Watch what the Wizard is doing . . . . . .Now the Wizard disappears, and in his place you see a Good Fairy . . . . . Is she carrying anything? . . . . . . What do you notice about her clothes? . . . . . What do you notice about her face? . . . . . What do you think she wants? . . . . . Do you hear any sounds? . . . . . Now the Good Fairy disappears . . . . . and in her place you see the Big Bad Wolf . . . . . Notice how he walks . . . . . Watch what he is doing . . . . . . Do you hear any sounds? . . . . . What do you think he wants? . . . . . Does he look like a wolf you might see in a forest, or is he different from that? . . . .

And now the Big Bad Wolf disappears and in his place you see the Superhero . . . . . Is he standing or sitting? What is he standing or sitting on? . . . . . Is he tall or short? . . . . . Is he dark or fair? . . . . . What is he wearing? . . . . . If he were looking for something, what do you think that might be? . . . . .

(For all students, continue the Visualization by using the following):

Now the stage clears and you see a Friendly Dog . . . . . . What color is his fur? . . . . Is it all one color, or is some of it different? . . . . Take a look at his ears-what shape and size are they? . . . . . Is he wagging his tail? Is it straight or curly? . . . . . As you watch this Friendly Dog, is he walking, or sitting, or lying down? . . . . .

Now the Friendly Dog disappears, and the lights on the stage turn yellow . . . . then orange . . . then red . . . then blue . . . and then they go out, and you come back here to this room, feeling the floor under your feet and the chair supporting you.

Grounding

Not yet, but in just a minute I will ask you to remove your blindfolds (or open your eyes). On your paper you have a total of eight squares: four on the front and four on the back.

(For primary students, just say "four squares.")

Your job is to describe a different character in each of the squares. You may either draw the character, or write words or sentences to describe the character. Or, if you wish, you may draw a picture and then add words to further describe or explain the character.

Please label each picture with the name of the character. I will put up this chart to refresh your memory. Some of you may not have a chance to complete all the squares. You may fill all of the squares, or just concentrate on a few.

Remove the blindfolds now. Please raise your hand if you have any questions, and I will come to your desk.

As usual, circulate during this time, clarifying directions and encouraging students in their work. From this point, it is not so important that you always make a drawing with your students.

Sharing

Ask each student to show or read a description of one of the characters. It is fun, after one student has described an archetype, to ask how many others saw some of the same details and characteristics. Share the term *archetype* with your students and point out that we all have images for archetypes inside our heads. This visualization is not as personal as the memories were, so you can begin to call on students who have not previously shared.

Evaluation

With this exercise, begin to give students more feedback about the effort you want them to put forth. You might wish to begin to give evaluations with a check or a point system. Give a plain check if the student has done about the expected amount of work, a plus mark if the student has done more work than expected, and a minus if the work is minimal. With a point system, you could give 1 for minimal, 2 for expected, and 3 for extra work. This evaluation is based solely on the effort the students made in translating their images into pictures and words.

Archetypes' Dwellings

Materials Needed

For each student:

- ✎ Art paper
- ✎ Pencil
- ✎ Blindfold

For the teacher:

- ✎ A chart, on the chalkboard or paper, with the names of archetypes: Big Bad Wolf, Wicked Witch, Beautiful Princess, Superhero

Preparation

- Tell students they will be working with archetypes again, some the same and some new. Their job will be to get a feeling for the predictability of certain kinds of characters. With older students, you might discuss what we mean when we say someone acted "out of character."

- Distribute materials. For primary only, have students fold their paper in half, open it out, and label each square in small print with the name of an archetype copied from your list.

- Show them how to use the front and back (two on front; two on back)

- Tell students that today they may use the blindfolds or merely close their eyes and keep them closed when signaled. Give them the responsibility of choosing the way that helps them get the clearest and most consistent images.

- Dim lights as a signal for students to put on blindfolds or shut their eyes.

Relaxation

First, put your feet flat on the floor and begin to relax and center yourself . . . . Move your shoulders and arms and hands as you wish to center yourself in gravity . . . Remember that you want gravity to do the main job of holding you upright . . . . Now put your hands on your desk if they are not there already . . . . And take a deep breath, all the way in . . . . and all the way out . . . . Once more, all the way in . . . . And all the way out .

Now return to the place that you created in your imagination yesterday . . . the place where you enjoy being alone . . . the place where you feel completely safe and comfortable . . . Feel yourself in that place . . . . Notice the sights you see . . . . . . and the sounds you hear . . . . . and the things that you can feel there . . . . . Take a moment to enjoy this place . . . . If you like to walk here . . . or run . . . or climb . . . or swim . . . or sit . . . anything that you would like to do to explore or experience this place you may do now . . . . Now please return to the place where you saw the stage before and take a seat before it . . . . Again take notice of its size and color; it might be the same as yesterday or quite different . . . . Again the curtains are closed . . . . The lights in the sky or the room are growing dim, and the stage lights are being turned on . . . . Make yourself comfortable and get ready to see what the characters are going to do today . . . .

Visualization

Now look at the stage . . . . . the curtain is about to part . . . . . As it parts the stage is not well lit, and you cannot see the scenery yet . . . . . but here comes the Beautiful Princess . . . . . She is walking across the stage . . . . Notice what she is wearing . . . . . What color is her hair? . . . . . Is she carrying anything? . . . . .

The Beautiful Princess is looking for her home, and as she walks across the stage, the light gets stronger and you can see her home there at the back of the stage . . . . . she sees it too, and she slowly walks toward it . . . . . . Watch her walk to her home; look at it carefully, so that you could draw it later . . . . What is it made of? . . . . . What color is it? . . . . . What shape are the windows? . . . . How many windows are there? . . . . . Can you see the roof? . . . . . How about the door—what does it look like? . . . . . How does it open as the Beautiful Princess walks through?

Watch the door close behind the Beautiful Princess as she enters her home and the stage lights grow dim once more. . . . . Here comes our next character, the Big Bad Wolf . . . . .What color is his fur? . . . . .What is his tail doing? . . . . .Is he walking slowly or quickly? . . . . .Is his head up or down? . . . . .

The Big Bad Wolf is looking for something, too — he is searching for his home. . . . . .Watch him search the stage, and slowly as the light grows stronger, you watch him find his home. . . . . .

Take a look at the Big Bad Wolf's home. . . . .What is it made of? . . . . .How tall or how short is it? . . . . .Is there a door for him to use, or is it a hole? . . . . .Watch the Big Bad Wolf as he circles around outside his home, and then goes inside for the night. . . . .Again, the stage lights grow dim and you can't see any scenery, but here comes another character—The Wicked Witch.

Watch the Wicked Witch as she looks for her home. . . . .What is the Wicked Witch wearing? . . . . . .Is she carrying anything with her? . . . . .Now she looks over and sees her home, and as the lights grow stronger you can begin to see it, too. As the witch walks toward her home, take a look at it. What color is it? How tall or how short is it? What do the windows look like? Is there a path leading up to the door? What kind of door does the witch's home have? . . . . . Watch it open, and see the Wicked Witch walk inside, tired after a long day of witch work. . . . As the door closes behind her, the lights dim again and her home fades out of sight. . . . .

Here comes one more character—the Superhero. Look and see what the Superhero is wearing. . . . .Is he carrying anything with him? . . . . .He walks across the stage looking for his own special home. . . . .There it is. . . . .Watch as the Superhero walks up to his home to go inside. . . . . . What color is it? What shape? . . . . .Are there windows? . . . . .What are they made of? . . . . .How tall or short is the Superhero's home? . . . . .Notice the doors—what are they made of? . . . . .And now the doors open and the Superhero goes inside, and the curtains on the stage slowly close. Take a nice, deep breath. . . . .

Grounding

For primary:

Please do not open your eyes yet, or take off the blindfolds. In just a minute, I want you to draw and write something on your papers. You already have a square for each of the characters on today's journey. Draw each of the four homes as you imagined them, one in each of the four squares, two on the front and two on the back. You may add any words you wish to label or describe each home. Begin.

For intermediate and upper:

Please do not open your eyes yet, or take off the blindfolds. In just a minute, I want you to draw and write something. You can choose to draw or write about all four of the dwellings, or to concentrate on one. If you wish to do all four, fold your paper in half. Use the front and back of your paper to draw and/or write about all four, two on the front and two on the back. If you wish to concentrate on one home, use the whole front of the paper to draw and the back to write about it further. Be sure to include the name of each archetype with each home. Begin.

Sharing

Invite students to talk about what they saw for each of the four homes. It is fun to ask how many students see similar elements for the same home. You can then explain more about the concept of archetypes, that they are forms or patterns for certain types of folk characters that we all see similarly and that are found in ancient stories from all around the world.

Evaluation

As before, page 49.

Extended Activities for Archetypes

Here are some ideas for creating new Journeys with the archetypes. You may use the same relaxation exercises that I used in this section, ending up with the appearance of the stage.

For maximum effectiveness, write your visualizations out in full script form, and practice with the tape recorder before working with your class.

Archetypes' Picnics

Name six archetypes, one by one. Allow time for students to visualize what each archetype would plan for a picnic. Visualize friends, food, equipment, vehicle, games, and location.

Students draw the picnic of one of the archetypes. Include the setting, the people, the food, the games, everything remembered. Students could list all of the elements of the picnic if they would rather write than draw.

Archetypes' Fears

Select six archetypes to call to the stage, one by one. Students imagine one thing that the archetype hopes will never happen. Allow students 20 seconds to see what the event is.

Students write each archetype's name and below it write the one thing that he or she hopes will never happen.

Archetypes' Goose

Pick six archetypes. One by one, watch to see what each will do when he or she finds the goose that lays the golden eggs. Give the students 20 seconds with each archetype to let the story unfold.

Tell students to list each archetype and what he or she does with the goose that lays the golden eggs. Then, write out the story of one of the archetypes and the magic goose.

5
Characters and Settings

Description

Students will visualize while you read descriptions of characters and settings. The characters' movement and speech will also be introduced in the reading.

Materials Needed

For each student:

- ✎ Paper
- ✎ Pencil
- ✎ Crayons
- ✎ Blindfold (optional)

For the teacher:

- ✎ A five- to ten-minute passage from a favorite book for each lesson. You may choose readings from the following list of books on which the Visualization and Grounding Activities section is based: *Ben and Me* by Robert Lawson, *Mrs. Frisby and the Rats of N.I.M.H* by Robert C. O'Brien, *Where the Red Fern Grows* by Wilson Rawls, *Stuart Little* by E. B. White, *The Black Pearl* by Scott O' Dell, *Across Five Aprils* by Irene Hunt, *Time at the Top* by Edward Ormondroyd, and *Black Beauty* by Anna Sewell.

Scheduling

- ➤ **Now:** 30 minutes for two days only for older students now. Later on, this idea could be adapted for primary with age-appropriate books.

- ➤ **Later in the year:** Do this on a regular basis, once every few weeks, to keep the skill of visualization alive.

Purpose

These exercises, using real descriptions of characters and settings from literature, teach your students to create these elements from books and stories in their minds' eyes so that their own reading will come fully alive.

Rationale

The following exercises are designed to ensure that your students will experience literature filled with three-dimensional people and places. If students identify literary characters only by name and not by physical and emotional characteristics, much of the nuance of the plot is lost.

At first glance, this activity may not seem much different from regular oral reading. In many classrooms, teachers read stories to their students daily. The difference here is that before you read, you will tell your students what they are to picture while you read and what they will be expected to do with those pictures when you are finished. This anticipatory set helps your students to tune in on the kind of visualizing they should do on a regular basis in their own reading. Do not let your students do anything except listen while you read the following exercises.

Preparations for Each Lesson

- Tell students that you are going to read from a book while they close their eyes and visualize. Before you read, describe the Grounding Activity in detail, so that they will know what to create in their minds' eyes.

- Distribute the materials, and ask your students to put them inside their desks to eliminate distractions. Those who use blindfolds should keep them available.

- Dim the lights as a signal to close eyes or put on blindfolds.

Relaxation for Each Lesson

You may choose from among any of the relaxation exercises in the appendix, page 144.

Visualization and Grounding Activities

The following suggestions are included for the books listed previously. Read a bit more slowly than usual, pausing between sentences to allow ample time for visualization.

Always tell your students what they will be asked to do after the reading. They can then concentrate on developing the images they will need for a successful experience.

Black Beauty by Anna Sewell

The first paragraph of *Black Beauty* describes the pasture where the horse Black Beauty was born. Tell your students that you will read the whole paragraph through; invite them to get a clear mental image while you are reading. Then read it again, one sentence at a time, and after each sentence let students draw that much of the scene. When you have read the entire paragraph, students will have drawn the entire pasture scene.

Here is the read-aloud excerpt from *Black Beauty*:

The first place that I can well remember was a large pleasant meadow with a pond of clear water in it. Some shady trees leaned over it, and rushes and water-lilies grew at the deep end. Over the hedge on one side we looked into a plowed field, and on the other we looked over a gate at our master's house, which stood by the roadside; at the top of the meadow was a grove of fir trees, and at the bottom a running brook overhung by a steep bank.

After reading this, explain that the character talking is a colt.

Ben and Me by Robert Lawson

In chapter 2, the author describes the invention of the Franklin stove. Tell your students you are going to read the description and then ask them to draw a picture of their conception of the stove.

When the reading is finished, ask students to begin drawing immediately. If your class asks you to repeat your reading, that is acceptable, especially with a description as detailed as this one.

Mrs. Frisby and the Rats of N.I.M.H. by Robert C. O'Brien

The description of the entrance to the intelligent rats' burrow in the first few pages of the book is an excellent passage to read aloud to your class. Before you begin, let your students know that you will ask them to draw their conception of how that entrance looks from the outside.

After the reading, you might also ask them to list seven words that describe that entrance.

Where the Red Fern Grows by Wilson Rawls

The first pages of this book give a vivid description of an old stray hound that is being attacked by a pack of hunting dogs.

For the grounding activity, ask your students to write answers to questions you have created about the dog's appearance, personality, and other distinguishing features. Remember to prompt students to visualize, to go a step beyond the book's literal description.

Stuart Little by E. B. White

In the first chapter, Stuart descends into the drain on a string to rescue Mrs. Little's lost ring. Ask your students to describe the descent and the inside of the drain to a partner.

After reading this selection, you might also ask the partners to make a joint drawing.

The Black Pearl by Scott O'Dell

When you finish the description of the Manta Diablo, have students work in pairs and describe the creature to each other, using gestures to show its size. Suggest that one student ask questions of the partner who is describing the animal.

Across Five Aprils by Irene Hunt

Before you begin, ask your students to image in great detail the two characters as you read. Tell the students they are going to write a letter telling a friend that he or she is supposed to pick up the characters at the bus station. To help the friend identify the characters, the letter must contain detailed descriptions.

Read the description found in the beginning of the book of Ellen and her son Jethro.

Time at the Top by Edward Ormondroyd

Tell your students that they will be describing an unusual elevator to a friend. The description must be so clear that the friend cannot confuse it with any other elevator.

At the beginning of chapter 5 there is a detailed description of the elevator that figures prominently in the plot.

After you have read the selection, ask students to write their own description.

Sharing

This will vary with the grounding activity you select. Some grounding activities, such as describing what was imaged to a partner, have the sharing built in.

General Suggestions for Grounding Activities

When you select other books to read to your class, you might adapt some of the activities that follow, or create others closely related to your story.

- Ask students to list seven words that describe a character, physically and emotionally.

- Remember, the activities should always elicit more details than the text describes as students visualize beyond the written word.

- There are no right or wrong answers. Grounding activities should allow for much diversity and creativity.

Evaluation

Look for comprehension; give credit for full participation.

6
Create a Myth

Description

Students will be guided through a universal myth up to the point of climax. They will then be given time to visualize a resolution and finish the myth in writing.

Scheduling

➤ **Now:** 40–50 minutes a day for two days for older students only. This idea can be adapted for primary if you find a story that fits this format.

➤ **Later in the Year:** Stay alert for other powerful stories that you can use in this way (i.e. reading the story right up to a vital decision point and then letting students "watch" the ending with their minds' eyes and then write about it).

Rationale

The many valuable activities in this chapter help students gain a sense of plot resolution.

My students have greatly enjoyed these activities, and I have found that the depth and sensitivity of their writing during the grounding activities make this one of the top writing assignments of the school year.

According to Joseph Campbell (1949) in *Hero with a Thousand Faces*, a myth is a great deal more than just a story. He writes: "the symbols of mythology are not manufactured; they cannot be ordered, invented, or permanently suppressed. They are spontaneous productions of the psyche, and each bears within it, undamaged, the germ power of its source."

When guided to deal with these symbols and the universal questions raised by the characters and heroes in the myths, the students are elevated to hero status themselves and usually resolve the myth in a way that adds to their own personal strength and humanity.

Phaeton and Apollo

Materials Needed

For each student:

- Lined paper and pencils for writing
- Crayons and unlined paper for drawing
- Blindfold (optional)

Preparation

- Tell students to get ready for a mind movie.

- Distribute materials. Explain that you will read a story up to a point, and then they will finish it.

- Dim lights as a signal to put on blindfolds or close eyes.

Relaxation

Select any exercise from the appendix, page 144.

Visualization

Today on your journey you will go back long ago and far away to a small village in ancient Greece. Phaeton, a handsome young boy, just about your age, lives alone with his mother, whom he loves and honors.

But as much as he loves his mother, he cannot help but miss having a father. His friends and schoolmates often tease him, saying his father could not have loved him or his mother if he ran away from them.

His mother tells him that this is not true. His father loved her very much and would love him, too, if only he could, but his father is not a mortal. He is Apollo, one of the gods, and gods are not allowed to live with mortals, even if they fall in love with one. The gods must live together on Mount Olympus, where they can watch over the human race.

Apollo has a particularly important job. He pulls the sun across the sky every day in a golden chariot drawn by seven immortal horses. His work brings light to the world, allowing the crops to grow and the earth to flourish. He could not possibly leave that vital work to come and live in a small house in an insignificant village.

The next time Phaeton's friends taunt him about his missing father, he tells them his mother's story. They laugh. They do not believe that Phaeton is the son of a god. They all know that Apollo is the god who pulls the fiery chariot of the sun across the skies. Phaeton could not possibly be the son of this powerful god. Phaeton is embarrassed and angry at their disbelief. He decides to do something that will prove to them that he is truly the son of Apollo.

For several days he thinks about how to prove that Apollo is his father. Finally, he thinks of a plan. He decides to visit his father and ask to drive the sun-chariot across the sky. If his friends saw him driving the chariot that pulls the sun, they would know the truth of his words.

Phaeton travels down a dusty road, past poor homes . . . . . and rich homes . . . . He stops and eats lunch under some olive trees, tasting the sweet bread and yellow cheese . . . . At a well nearby, he pulls up water to drink and to wash off the dust of his travels . . . . . .

Soon after lunch, the path brings him to the foot of Mount Olympus, the home of the gods . . . It stretches high above.

The way to the palace of the sun is steep and awesome, but Phaeton is young and strong, and determined to succeed . . . . . Finally, he sees the palace in front of him . . . . .

As he approaches, the silver doors open to reveal a huge hall. The light from within is almost more than he can bear . . . . . The light is coming from a throne at the end of the hall, a throne made of gold encrusted with diamonds, and shining almost as brightly as the sun itself . . . . .

Seated on this magnificent throne is Apollo. He is robed in deepest purple and crowned with rubies and amethysts.

Apollo instantly recognizes his son and makes him welcome . . . . He asks Phaeton why he came on this long, hard journey. Phaeton explains the trouble that he had with his friends, and tells him that he has a favor to ask. Out of his deep love for his son, Apollo grants him any wish that he might have. Phaeton asks to drive the sun-chariot across the sky.

Apollo is thunderstruck. He begs Phaeton to reconsider, to ask him anything but that. Driving the sun-chariot is beyond the power of a mere mortal. The horses are almost too much for even Apollo to control. Should the chariot get out of control, it might go too low and scorch the earth, setting homes and fields on fire. If it should go too high, it would burn the heavens and the homes of the gods, and the earth would be left to freeze.

Even if Phaeton could keep the chariot on its course, there are terrible monsters that must be avoided: the wild bull, the archer, the lion, the scorpion, and the crab. It is dangerous beyond understanding.

But there is nothing else Phaeton wants as much as this one favor. His friends will know beyond any doubt that he is the child of Apollo if he drives the sun-chariot through the skies . . . . .

Once more Apollo begs his son to change his mind. He says that if Phaeton insists, he must keep his promise, but he will grant any other wish if Phaeton will just release him from his pledge. Phaeton knows that his father is right about the dangers of the journey, but the sky beckons and he remembers the taunts of his friends. What will he decide?

You have exactly one minute to imagine what Phaeton decides and what will happen next. Begin.

(Wait exactly one minute.)

Now bring the Journey to an end . . . . . . Bring your attention back to the classroom now, feeling your feet on the floor and your chair supporting you . . . . .

Grounding

In just a minute I will ask you to open your eyes. When it is time, I want you to write down what happened in your part of the story. Start at the place where Phaeton makes his decision about whether to insist on driving the sun's chariot across the sky. Write down everything that happened or was said from that moment on. If you finish early, illustrate your writing with pictures of what you saw.

If you have any questions, please raise your hand. Ready, begin.

This grounding activity will take quite a while for some students, as they will have a lot to write. Be sure to allow enough time. You can circulate and encourage the writing that clearly tells others about the writer's mental images.

Sharing

Collect and read the endings to the class. Students may or may not wish to acknowledge their authorship. This part of the activity will run over the hour allotted and so may need to be finished the next day.

Evaluation

Grade for effort (length, description, detail).

Pandora's Box

Materials Needed

For each student:

- ✎ Lined paper and pencils
- ✎ Unlined paper and crayons
- ✎ Blindfold (optional)

Preparation

- Tell students they will be finishing another story today, and to get their mind movies ready to go.

- Distribute materials.

- Dim lights as a signal to close eyes or put on blindfolds.

Relaxation

Use the same relaxation exercise as for Phaeton and Apollo, page 61.

Visualization

We are going to go long ago and far away to a time when the earth was inhabited by children alone. Even the earth is young and beautiful. There is no disease, no death, no disappointment. The children are happy all of the time. They dance . . . . . . they sing . . . . . they play in the meadows and streams . . . . . they pick the fruit off the trees for their food . . . . . and in these long-ago times the fruit grows all the year round, for there is no winter to end the growing season.

Today we are going to the house of a boy named Epimetheus. See his house at the edge of a meadow . . . . . Epimetheus is wishing for a companion. He asks the gods to send him someone to keep him company.

The gods hear his wish and decide to send Pandora to him. She is a lovely and gracious young girl who is pleased to hear that she will be the companion for this kind boy, Epimetheus. When she is ready to go, Mercury, with his winged cap and winged feet, comes to fly her through the air to her new home.

Under Mercury's arm she can't help but notice a very large and very interesting box. She is curious about what could be in this box, and so are you. But one can't bother the gods by asking them a lot of questions, so she decides that it is probably a gift for Epimetheus, and she will wait until she reaches his home to find out what it is.

Mercury picks her up as if she were no heavier than a pillow of goose down. Gently he flies her over the treetops and housetops . . . . . over the cows and sheep . . . . . over the lakes and streams . . . . . over the children happily playing at their games . . . . .

Soon you notice that Mercury is descending . . . . . . and there is a lovely little house that seems to be their destination . . . . . They touch the earth once more and Epimetheus comes out of the house, greeting Pandora and making her feel welcome at once . . . . . Mercury deposits the large box inside the house and makes ready to leave.

Pandora stops him, asking about the box. "Oh yes," answers Mercury. "I meant to tell you about that. Pandora, you and Epimetheus are to keep this box and guard it. But you are never to open it. Whatever happens, do not open the box."

Now Pandora does not know what is in this box or why the gods have given the box to her, but you must know the answers to those questions.

The gods were very angry with the human race. They didn't like to see all the children running around, living life as happily as the gods themselves. So they got together to figure out a way to punish humanity.

They decided to gather up a collection of nasty little black creatures called Troubles. There was one called Death, one called Jealousy, and one called Hatred. Lies, Cheating, Disease, Guilt, and Anger all were gathered up by the gods like so many buzzing insects, and all were put into the box.

But the gods began to feel a little sorry that they were bringing so much evil to the human race. They decided that at the very bottom of the box they would put a lovely, rainbow-winged creature called Hope. So in went Hope, last of all, where she took refuge in the corner at the bottom of the box. Then the gods gave the box to Mercury, who, in turn, gave it to Pandora and Epimetheus. Mercury and all the other gods were sure that Pandora would not long be able to keep from looking inside the box.

Ignorant of what the gods had planned, at first Pandora is hardly bothered by the presence of the box. There are new friends to meet and new places to see . . . . . As the days go by though, she begins to notice the box more and more. She begins to spend hours looking at it . . . . . wondering what treasure could possibly be contained inside . . . . . If it comes from the gods, it must be something wonderful . . . . . clothes of gold, or jewels . . . . .Why did Mercury give it to her if he didn't really want her to open it? . . . Perhaps, she thinks, Mercury wanted to test her bravery . . . Perhaps he hoped that she would have the courage to open it . . .

Oh, a hundred excuses run through her head, urging her to open the box.

While Epimetheus and the other children are out playing, she sits by the box, running her fingers over its surface. Notice what is the box is made of . . . . . Look at how it is fastened . . . . . It could easily be undone and opened . . . . One day, as Pandora sits near the box, overcome with curiosity, a tiny voice seems to come from inside the box, saying, "Pandora, let us out. Let us out. We want to play with you."

She is amazed. She thinks that they may be little elves, or perhaps caterpillars and butterflies. She cannot bear to think of living things trapped inside a dark old box. Her fingers go to the clasp, and almost without her effort, the clasp is undone all by itself.

Instantly, she regrets what she has done and tries to fasten the box together again, but she cannot. It is as if a part of the clasp were missing. She knows that when Epimetheus comes in from play and sees the box unfastened, he will think that she has already opened the lid and peeked inside.

Pandora decides that if Epimetheus will think she has peeked inside the box, then she might as well go ahead and do it. Her hand goes to the lid of the box. She pauses, hearing the children playing outside. The sunshine seems to be saying, "Why bother about that old box, Pandora? Come outside and play in the meadow with your friends."

Then she looks back at the box and thinks of the little voice inside, begging to be let out. She knows that if she does not open the box today, it will be there tomorrow and the next day and the next, always begging her to open it and end the suspense. (It's as if you knew where all your Christmas presents were hidden, but you aren't supposed to go and look.)

While she is trying to decide, Epimetheus comes into the house behind her. For a moment, at least, he doesn't make a move to stop her from opening the box. He stands quietly, watching to see what she will do.

Put yourself in Pandora's place, sitting by this box that is begging to be opened. What will you do?

You have exactly one minute to watch and see what you will do, and see what will happen next. Ready, begin.

(Wait exactly one minute.)

Now bring this to a close, finish up anything that you would like . . . . And bring your attention back to this room, with the floor beneath your feet and your desk supporting you.

Grounding

Not yet, but in just a minute I want you to write down what happened. First tell whether the box was opened or not, and then write down everything that happened and everything that was said. If you finish early, you may illustrate your story with any pictures that you saw in your mind's eye as the story unfolded. Do not talk until all of the work is done. If you have questions, raise your hand and I will come to your desk. Ready, begin.

Circulate and encourage good writing. Remember that this activity will take quite a while for some of your students.

Sharing

You can collect the papers and read the endings, ask for volunteers to read the endings, or pair up students and have them read their endings to each other.

Evaluation

Grade for effort (length, description, dialogue, details).

Section II

Reading with the Mind's Eye

The exercises in section I of this manual were aimed at encouraging students to see mental pictures through sensory stimulation and personal memories. Even after students are able to visualize, they do not necessarily do so when they are reading the printed word.

Once we have enabled students to readily use their minds' eyes, we need to turn our attention to encouraging the use of these mental pictures when our students are reading the printed word or while they are listening to a story being read aloud. The next section of this manual is designed to help your students make that vital link between visualizing and reading and writing.

How to Use This Section

This section is used most effectively after you have taken your whole class through the exercises in section I of this manual. However, if you are certain that your students are visualizing effectively, you can start the activities in this section simultaneously with any one of the visualization exercises from the first section that you may choose to use. If there is any reason that you would prefer to skip section I, you can also begin here, with the activities in section II.

Each exercise in this section stands alone and can be done whenever it fits with your curriculum. You can also mix the exercises found in this section with those in section III: Writing with the Mind's Eye. After you have done the first set of exercises, Image While You Read, there is no particular order in which the rest of the exercises in this manual need to occur. Each strategy stands on its own.

7

Image While You Read

Description

A folktale is presented with just a paragraph or two on each of ten pages, with blank areas for student illustration. You will question small groups of students for details of their visualization as they read one page each day. Press for much detail in everyone's visual images in order to teach all students to generate vivid pictures from their reading. Students then illustrate the pages by drawing one of their mental images each day. Over a two-week period, the entire story is visualized and illustrated by each individual student, culminating in a completed book for each student and greatly improved visualization skills.

Materials Needed

For each student:

- ✎ A teacher-made folktale book (see Preparation)
- ✎ Crayons or felt-tipped pens
- ✎ 5-inch by 8-inch index card to cover the text

For the teacher:

- ✎ A list of questions about the story that cannot be answered from information in the text alone, questions that stretch the mind's eye. Questions for *The Farmer Who Bought a Dream* are included.

Scheduling

- ➤ **Now:** 10–15 minutes a day for two weeks for each small group of five to six students at all grade levels

- ➤ **Later in the year:** One two-week session with this format should get all of your students visualizing while they read, and you will not have to repeat it with the same intensity of questioning. It is fun, however, to create these self-illustrated books for many different stories, especially at the primary level. You can repeat this exercise with new stories that you discover. (Laura Rose's book *Folktales* has ten more stories set up like this.) You can also use the same strategy with poems, as described in chapter 9, page 89.

Purpose

This is where we directly link students' ability to visualize with the act of reading.

This is an absolutely essential set of exercises to do at all grade levels.

If your older students are reluctant to read a simple folktale like this one, have them complete the illustration of their individual books for *The Farmer Who Bought a Dream* and take them to a primary classroom to read to a partner, then leave the books behind as a study-buddy present. This will imbue the activity with importance, and perhaps overcome any reluctance to read the kind of simple, short story that is necessary for this activity.

Rationale

If we hope to turn poor readers into good readers, we must make a concentrated effort to teach them exactly how to visualize while reading. We need to bring together students' abilities to visualize with their ability to decode so that they will begin fully to see and comprehend what they are reading.

The exercises in this chapter are extraordinarily helpful for any students who are having trouble with reading or visualizing. This chapter can also be used with first graders in the spring, when they are able to do some reading, to get beginning readers off to a good start in visualizing while they read.

In this chapter, you will teach your students to see detailed pictures of exactly what they are reading. Continuing the exercises over a period of two weeks accustoms students to the process of visualizing while reading. Children who are discouraged about reading find these exercises to be strong confidence builders; this is a very low-risk format because there are no wrong answers.

Preparation

Before the lesson:

- Create a book for each student by cutting out the ten sections of "The Farmer Who Bought a Dream" from pages 80–84, by attaching each of the ten sections along the bottom of an $8^1/_2$-inch x 11-inch sheet of copy paper. (The first page is already set up as an example of the way you will attach the nine sections that follow it.) Then, on a copy machine, duplicate all ten pages for each of your students. Staple the pages together with a blank cover page for the title and author, and let students write their own names as the illustrator of their copy.

- Arrange your class in heterogeneous groups of five or six students each (for example, one low reader, two or three middle, and one high).

- Plan work for the rest of your class to do while you meet with each small group for ten to fifteen minutes each day for two weeks.

Starting the lesson:

- Give the class some independent work, and gather one group of five or six students together.

- Give them their copies of the story and an index card. (For older students you might prefer to give them only a page a day so that no eager beavers will read ahead.)

Visualization: Day 1

Instruct the group to cover all text but the first three lines. Read these aloud, asking students to shut their eyes and imagine as you read.

> One autumn day in a valley in far-off Japan, a farmer and his neighbor went into the forest to gather some firewood for the winter. After a while, the two men grew tired from working, so they stretched out to rest on the soft orange and yellow leaves that had fallen from the trees.

Now you will begin to ask questions that are meant to elicit strong visual images from every student. If you have already done some exercises from section I, this should be easy to do.

If you are beginning your visualization training with this set of exercises, it will take more effort, more encouragement, and more time. Be patient. If a student says, "I don't know," say something like, "Then close your eyes and look and I will get back to you in just a minute." If the student still has trouble, give hints and suggestions: Did they use a saw? An axe? Show me with your hands how big it was. What color was the handle?

Begin by asking each student in the group specific questions about the mental images that he or she sees. Press for details not included in the text. Include questions about time of day, landscape, colors, feelings, weather, size, predictions, sounds, smells, anything at all that will lead students to use their imaginations. Involve as many senses as possible, because different children have stronger connections with different senses.

Ask many students the same questions without making the exercise tedious, and encourage many different answers to the same question. You are trying to get each student to create a vivid and individual image from the text.

Here are some questions you might ask on day one:

What are the men wearing? What colors are their clothes? Are they wearing anything on their heads? On their feet?

What color is their hair? Their eyes?

How many trees do you see? Do they still have leaves on them? What color are the tree trunks?

How did the men break up the firewood? What did they use? Show me how big it was. How big around was the firewood?

What color are the leaves that the men stretched out on? Can you see the forest floor too, or do the leaves cover it all up?

When a student answers one question, follow up with another question that presses the student to see even more vividly. For instance, if you ask what color the man's hair is and the student says black, then ask how long the hair is, and whether it is straight or curly, and what about the other man's hair.

Accept all answers unless they make no sense at all. If later text makes a student's initial pictures invalid, then discuss with your students how we must keep changing our pictures as we get more information.

After about ten minutes, read the rest of the text on this page and ask a few questions about it.

> The neighbor fell fast asleep the minute his head touched the ground, and soon he was snoring away, "Zzzzzzzzzzzzz."
>
> Not long after, the farmer dozed off as well.

Now, have all of the students read the entire passage on page 1 aloud with you. This repetition will help nearly every beginning and struggling reader learn to read this story by the end of the ten days.

Grounding

Tell students to illustrate this page by drawing any of the images that they saw. Even students who are reluctant to draw can do something as simple as drawing just the axe or a leaf or two. I have found, however, that most students draw very detailed illustrations after they have vividly visualized.

You can work with another group while this group draws. Then collect the text so that students won't read ahead before tomorrow.

Sharing

Students may informally discuss each other's drawings during the drawing period, but formal sharing will take place on the last day.

Visualization: Day 2

For primary:

Have all students read along with you as you reread yesterday's page. Then ask them to read along silently or close their eyes to visualize while you read page 2.

For intermediate and upper grades:

Either read aloud or let all students read the previous day's text silently. If you do the latter, it would be a good idea to meet with your lowest readers individually before this session to have each of them read page 1 aloud to you. This facilitates a fresh attempt to make reading work for them.

Proceed with page 2 just as you did with page 1. Read the first paragraph.

When they awoke, the neighbor told the farmer that he had dreamed an amazing dream. "In my dream I saw a pot filled with all the gold a heart could desire. The pot was hidden in the dirt, and the dirt was under a tree, and the tree was on a hill, and the hill was near the house of the richest man in the entire city of Osaka!"

Then ask many questions about the neighbor's dream to elicit vivid mental pictures, such as:

Take a look at the pot: What shape is it? What color is it? What is it made of? Does it have a lid? Can you see anything in it or is the inside hidden?

If you can see the gold, what shape is it? Is it in pieces—how big are the pieces? How many pieces do you see?

The pot is hidden under a tree—what does the tree look like? Which way do the branches point, up or down? Are there leaves? What color are they? Are there any leaves on the ground beneath the tree? What color are they?

The tree is near a rich man's house—can you describe the house? What color is it? Does it have windows? What about the door—what color is the door? What is the house made of?

Then read the rest of the page and discuss it, too.

"That is an amazing dream," replied the farmer. "I tell you, neighbor, you should go to Osaka this very day and follow your dream. You never know where a dream might lead you."

But the neighbor didn't think much of the idea of following a dream, certainly not if it would take him all the way to Osaka. He just laughed and said that it was only a foolish dream.

There are not nearly as many visual images in this part of the text, so discuss it more briefly. Here are a few starting questions, then follow the students' lead:

How does the farmer look as he is telling his neighbor to follow his dream? What is he doing with his body, or his arms? What expression is on his face?

When the neighbor listens to the farmer, what expression does he show? Make your body look the way you think the neighbor is holding his body as he listens to his friend's words. Why do you think he doesn't want to follow his dream? What do you suppose he is thinking about his friend, the farmer, who wants him to follow his dream all the way to Osaka?

How far do you think Osaka might be? How many days could it take to walk there?

Now have all the students read this page aloud with you. This repetition will help nearly every beginning and struggling reader learn to read this story by the end of the ten days.

Grounding

Tell students to illustrate this page by drawing any of the images that they saw. You can work with another group while this group draws. Then collect the text.

 ## Visualization: Day 3

For primary:

Have all students read along with you as you reread the first two pages. Then ask them to read along silently or close their eyes to visualize while you read page 3.

For older students:

Review as before. Then proceed with page 3 just as you did with page 1 and 2. Today, read the entire page before discussing it.

The two men finished chopping the firewood and loading it onto their backs to carry home, but the farmer couldn't forget the dream about the pot filled with all the gold a heart could desire. Again he urged his neighbor to go and look for the gold that filled the pot that was hidden in the dirt that was under a tree that was on a hill that was near the house of the richest man in the entire city of Osaka! But again, the neighbor laughed and called the dream foolish. So finally, the farmer offered to buy his neighbor's dream.

"What! Buy my dream?" asked the neighbor. "I've never heard of such foolishness. No one in all of Japan has ever heard of such foolishness!"

Well, they argued back and forth for a while, one saying this and the other saying that, but before they reached home, the farmer had bought the dream, and that was that.

Some questions:

How did the men get the wood onto their backs? Did each put his own wood there, or did they help each other? How did the wood stay there? Was there a cord? What was it made of? Was there a sack? How big was it? How many pieces of wood did they carry? Was the wood straight or crooked? Show me with your hands: how big around were the pieces?

What did the farmer use to buy the dream? Where was he carrying the payment? How much did he pay?

Remember the path they were walking on to get home. Was it straight or crooked? Were they in the woods all the way home, or did they leave the woods? If they left, what was the country like outside of the woods? Was it flat or did the road go up and down? Were there stones, or dirt, or pavement? How long did they walk?

Have all of the students read this page aloud with you.

Grounding

As before, page 76.

 ## Visualization: Day 4

As before, read or review the story up until now. Then read today's page.

The next morning the farmer sat down to talk with his wife.

"Wife," he said, "while I was in the woods yesterday, our neighbor had the most amazing dream. He dreamt of a pot filled with all the gold a heart could desire. The pot was hidden in the dirt, and the dirt was under a tree, and the tree was on a hill, and the hill was near the house of the richest man in the entire city of Osaka."

"That's a very nice dream, dear," said the wife.

"But that's not all," said the farmer. "Since our neighbor did not want to follow his dream, I bought it from him, and I must be off to Osaka."

"What! You bought a dream?" exclaimed the poor wife. "And you must be off to Osaka? What foolishness is this? I've never heard of such foolishness. No one in all of Japan has ever heard of such foolishness!"

The farmer tried to explain, and the wife tried to understand. But in the end the farmer went off to Osaka and the wife, shaking her poor head, picked up her children and went off to see her mother.

Continue as on previous days. Some questions:

What does the wife look like? Is she taller or shorter than the farmer? What is she wearing? What color are her clothes? What else do you notice about her? What is on her feet? Is anything on her head? What color is her hair? How long is her hair?

When the farmer sits down to talk with his wife, what does he sit on? Describe it to me so I can see it too.

What was the wife doing when the farmer sat down to talk with her? (Follow up on this answer with requests for more details.)

How many children do the farmer and his wife have? Show me with your hands how tall they are. What are they wearing? What is on their feet?

Read this page together.

Grounding

As before, page 76.

Visualization: Days 5–9

Each day continue as before. (The story in its entirety can be found at the end of this chapter.) Invent questions that invite vivid, detailed imaging.

Sharing: Day 10

When the story is complete, do the following:

For primary:

Have students read the entire book to a partner; next have both students sign the back of each other's book. Ask the students to find another partner and read the book once again. Do this with five or six partners to get in lots of reading practice. Then send the book home with students to read to a parent for homework, and ask the parent to sign the back of the book.

For older students (optional):

Have students go to a primary classroom and read their stories to the children there. You might even have them leave the books with their reading partners as a gift, or give them to the teacher to add to the classroom library.

The Farmer Who Bought a Dream

One autumn day in a valley in far-off Japan, a farmer and his neighbor went into the forest to gather some firewood for the winter. After a while, the two men grew tired of working, so they stretched out to rest on the soft orange and yellow leaves that had fallen from the trees.

The neighbor fell fast asleep the minute his head touched the ground, and soon he was snoring away, *"Zzzzzzzzzzzz."*

Not long after, the farmer dozed off as well.

Day Two

When they awoke, the neighbor told the farmer that he had dreamed an amazing dream. "In my dream I saw a pot filled with all the gold a heart could desire. The pot was hidden in the dirt, and the dirt was under a tree, and the tree was on a hill, and the hill was near the house of the richest man in the entire city of Osaka!"

"That is an amazing dream," replied the farmer. "I tell you, neighbor, you should go to Osaka this very day and follow your dream. You never know where a dream might lead you."

But the neighbor didn't think much of the idea of following a dream, certainly not if it would take him all the way to Osaka. He just laughed and said that it was only a foolish dream.

Day Three

The two men finished chopping the firewood and loading it onto their backs to carry home, but the farmer couldn't forget the dream about the pot filled with all the gold a heart could desire. Again he urged his neighbor to go and look for the gold that filled the pot that was hidden in the dirt that was under a tree that was on a hill that was near the house of the richest man in the entire city of Osaka! But again, the neighbor laughed and called the dream foolish. So finally, the farmer offered to buy his neighbor's dream.

"What! Buy my dream?" asked the neighbor. "I've never heard of such foolishness. No one in all of Japan has ever heard of such foolishness!"

Well, they argued back and forth for a while, one saying this and the other saying that, but before they reached home, the farmer had bought the dream, and that was that.

Day Four

The next morning the farmer sat down to talk with his wife.

"Wife," he said, "while I was in the woods yesterday, our neighbor had the most amazing dream. He dreamt of a pot filled with all the gold a heart could desire. The pot was hidden in the dirt, and the dirt was under a tree, and the tree was on a hill, and the hill was near the house of the richest man in the entire city of Osaka."

"That's a very nice dream, dear," said the wife.

"But that's not all," said the farmer. "Since our neighbor did not want to follow his dream, I bought it from him, and I must be off to Osaka."

"What! You bought a dream?" exclaimed the poor wife. "And you must be off to Osaka? What foolishness is this? I've never heard of such foolishness. No one in all of Japan has ever heard of such foolishness!"

The farmer tried to explain, and the wife tried to understand. But in the end the farmer went off to Osaka and the wife, shaking her poor head, picked up her children and went off to see her mother.

Day Five

Now the city of Osaka was many miles away from the farmer's little home, and he had to travel for seven days and seven nights. He slept by the side of the road. He gathered food when he could and went hungry when he could not. At last, he reached the city, found the house of the richest man, and knocked on the door.

After a time, the richest man opened his elegant door, and the farmer told him his story. The farmer explained how his neighbor had dreamed of a pot filled with all the gold a heart could desire. The pot was hidden in the dirt, and the dirt was under a tree, and the tree was on a hill, and the hill was near the house of the richest man in the entire city of Osaka!

Then the farmer explained that he had bought this dream and followed it all the way to Osaka. He asked the rich man most politely if he might dig for the pot of gold. Of course the farmer offered to share whatever he might find.

Day Six

The rich man was very surprised to hear this dream, because he knew nothing of a pot hidden in the dirt, under a tree, on a hill near his house.

To the farmer, the rich man said, "Please do me the honor of resting here in my house for the night, and in the morning I will have my servants help you dig for the pot of gold. We will share everything you find."

But to himself, the rich man said, "This is certainly a most amazing dream! But why should I let this farmer have what is buried under my tree and on my hill next to my house?"

So, after the farmer had been fed and tucked into a comfortable bed, this greedy rich man and his servants took their shovels and slipped behind the house.

Day Seven

The midnight moon shone on the servants as they dug in the dirt that was under the tree that was on the hill that was near the house of the richest man in the entire city of Osaka. As soon as the pot was uncovered, the rich man pushed his servants aside and eagerly lifted the lid.

Instantly, the man was knocked to the ground as something rushed out from the pot with a sound like thunder. Ba jaba jaba jaba jaba jaba jaba jaba. Whatever had come out of the pot disappeared completely into the night sky, for by the time the rich man got back on his feet and peeked into the pot, there was nothing at all inside.

Day Eight

The next morning the servants took the farmer out to the hill to dig for gold. When the farmer dug up the pot, he was excited because the dream was coming true. But as you know, and as the rich man had already discovered, there was nothing at all inside the pot.

The farmer could not believe his eyes. Every part of the dream had been true. The pot was hidden in the dirt that was under the tree that was on the hill that was near the house of the richest man in Osaka. But the pot was empty! His wife had been right. His neighbor had been right. He was a fool to buy a dream. He was the most foolish man in all of Japan.

Day Nine

The farmer thanked the rich man for his help and sadly started home. After spending seven days and seven nights on the road, gathering food when he could and going hungry when he could not, the farmer at last saw his own little house over the next hill. As he walked closer and closer, he tried to think of what he could say to his wife about his following such a foolish dream.

But as he came near the little house, his children ran out, shouting, "To-chan! To-chan!" (which means, "Papa! Papa!"). "Come and see what has fallen from the sky while you were gone!"

To the farmer's great surprise, his wife ran toward him and threw her arms around him. She was smiling from ear to ear. "Oh, husband, husband, just wait until you see!" she cried. "Seven nights ago, just after midnight, we were all awakened from our sleep by a sound like thunder. Ba jaba jaba jaba jaba jaba jaba jaba. Then gold coins came flying through the sky to our house. They came in through the windows. They came in through the doors. They came in through the chimney, until the whole floor of our little house was shining with gold. Pika, Pika, Pika, Pika, Pika, Pika, Pika. Your dream has come true!"

Day Ten

So the farmer walked in through the door, and sure enough, gold lay thick on the floor in the front room, and in the kitchen, and in every room of that little house.

Now it is never possible to explain a miracle. But I think that the gold was meant to be owned by someone like that farmer, someone who could follow a dream with courage and a fair heart. The neighbor was a nice fellow, but he had no imagination, so he couldn't follow his dream. And the rich man was not only greedy, but down-right dishonest. So when the rich man opened the pot, well, you all saw what must have happened.

I am delighted to tell you that the farmer and his family lived happily ever after. And it is probably no surprise to you that they shared their happiness with all of their neighbors, and that no one in their valley ever went hungry or cold again.

8

Picture Book Images

(For primary grades)

Description

After you read a story without showing the book's illustrations, students draw their own images of what the author is communicating.

Materials Needed

For each student:

- ✎ Art paper
- ✎ Crayons or felt-tipped pens

For the teacher:

- ✎ A picture book with a strong story line
- ✎ Occasionally, use a recorded version of a story

Scheduling

➤ **At any time after students are reading and visualizing:** About 30 minutes for each picture book that you choose to do for primary grades.

Preparation

- Select a picture book that evokes particularly vivid mental images, such as one from the list starting on page 86.

- Pass out art paper and crayons or felt-tipped pens

Visualization

- Tell the students that today you are not going to show the pictures as you read the story. (After the entire lesson is finished, you may show the pictures.) You want the students to make their own pictures with their wonderful minds' eyes.

- Tell students that at the end of the story, you will ask them to draw the very best picture that they can create. As you read, stop fairly often, and ask students to shut their eyes and get a picture. While their eyes are shut, ask questions that will lead students to picture details such as the kind and color of the clothes the characters are wearing. Stop often enough to stimulate the development of mental pictures, but not often enough to ruin the flow of the story. In this, your art comes into play.

Grounding

When you have finished the story, ask students to shut their eyes and see their favorite part. Tell them that as soon as they have a really clear picture, they are quietly to draw it. As students finish their drawings, direct them to write the words that tell what is happening. Help them with the spelling, so that everyone can read their captions.

Sample Stories

1. *Joey* by Jack Kent. A mother kangaroo is so protective of her child, Joey, that she will let him play with his friends only if he stays in her pouch. Soon her pouch is full of friends, drums, stereos, and even a piano.

   - Pass out art materials and tell students to set them aside.

   - Read *Joey* without showing the students the illustrations; instead, encourage mental pictures along the way. Stop just before the mother says, "That will do," and kicks everyone out. Ask your students to draw the pouch as it looks at this point in the story. When they finish drawing, they can add a caption or a comment to describe their pictures.

   - After allowing a few minutes for drawing, reread and finish the story. Students may continue drawing as you read. When all your students have completed their drawings, you could show the author's illustrations.

2. *Abiyoyo* with text by Pete Seeger. This is a free adaptation of an African folktale about a little boy who conquers a giant with a song and saves his village. The giant is described in vivid detail.

- Pass out art materials and tell students to set them aside.

- Read or tell the entire story. At the end, have your students draw the giant as they saw him. They may also draw the boy, his father, or anything else in the story, but the main subject must be the giant. Extra long paper makes this an even more exciting drawing adventure.

- After the students have been drawing for a while, reread and finish the story. Show the original illustrations, if you wish.

3. *How to Get Rid of Bad Dreams* by Nancy Hazbry and Roy Condy. In this book, bad dream monsters are neutralized by the inventive thinking of the dreamer. A monster is scared away by the quick use of a mirror, as he is frightened by his own image. A dragon is shrunk by a laser, and presto, the dreamer is the only kid in school with a pet dragon in her pocket.

- Pass out art materials and have students set them aside.

- Read the whole book without showing the illustrations, then ask the students to imagine a dream monster. Invite them to share what they see. Next, have them see a silly or funny situation happen to change their monster. Use and discuss the word *transformation.*

- Ask children individually to tell you how the monster was transformed before you release each one to the drawing area. Help those who have no ideas with suggestions of your own. Tell students to write a caption on their picture that tells how the transformation took place. You might give them the frame sentence: If I dream about a _____, I could _____.

- Collect the drawings and make a class book. Students love to hear you read their captions aloud, and they enjoy reading and rereading the class book on their own.

4. *A Boat for Peppe* by Leo Politi. This is the story of a boy in a fishing village who longs for a toy boat of his own. At the story's end, an old man has made for Peppe the boat of his dreams.

- Pass out art materials and have students set them aside.

- Read the whole story to your class. You may show some of the illustrations in the book if you like, but do not show the illustrations of the boat that Peppe is given by his friend.

- When you finish the story, ask students to draw the boat that Peppe received, and to add a caption or comment.

5. *William's Doll* by Charlotte Zolotow. This is a charming story of a boy who wants a doll. His father buys the boy every toy but the doll, but his grandmother gets him what he wants because, as she tells his father, the boy needs to learn how to take care of a baby so that he can be a good father himself someday.

- Pass out art materials and have students set them aside.

- Read the book to your class. You may show some illustrations if you wish, but do not show the doll William eventually is given.

- Have your students draw the doll that they imagine William gettting. You might ask them to write a prediction about how they think William will treat the doll or about what kind of a father he will grow up to be and why.

Sharing

Students can gather in pairs or small groups to share what they have drawn and written. Sometimes it is appropriate to create a class book with the drawings; you can read this book to the children and then put it in the class library.

Evaluation

Look for comprehension; grade for effort.

9

Creating Images with Poetry Books

(For primary grades)

Description

Students illustrate a class book of a poem they have memorized. Each line of the poem is illustrated on a separate page.

Materials Needed

- ✎ 9-inch by 12-inch sheets of white construction paper
- ✎ 2 sheets of colored (preferably laminated) paper
- ✎ Crayons or felt-tipped pens
- ✎ Pencils

Scheduling

➤ **At any time after students are reading and visualizing:** 30–45 minutes for primary only.

Purpose

Students further develop their visualization skills with the rich, descriptive language of poetry. At the same time, their appreciation of descriptive poetry deepens. Primary students learn to read these poems independently by using this strategy.

Rationale

Children love to read and reread the poems that they have memorized and then illustrated. This provides self-motivating reading practice for beginning readers. When students take time to vividly visualize a poem that they have memorized, their illustrations tend to be rich and amazingly detailed, providing pleasure for themselves and their classmates.

Preparation

Before the lesson:

- Select a poem of no more than 10–12 lines, each line of which gives a strong visual image, as in:

> *Rain on the green grass*
> *Rain on the trees,*
> *Rain on the rooftops,*
> *But not on me!*
>> —Anonymous

Or

> *1, 2, buckle my shoe,*
> *3, 4, shut the door,*
> *5, 6, pick up sticks,*
> *7, 8, lay them straight,*
> *9, 10, a big fat hen.*
>> —Traditional

I usually pick short poems because I expect all of my students to memorize them.

Copyright restrictions prevent me from including more poems in this manual for you, but here is a list of poems I have found to be well adapted to this activity. They are all taken from *Read-Aloud Rhymes for the Very Young* (1986).

- "Footnote" by Norah Smaridge
- "Holding Hands" by Lenore M. Link
- "Rainy Day" by William Wise
- "The Little Turtle" by Vachel Lindsay
- "The Frog on the Log" by Ilo Orleans
- "The Very Nicest Place" Anonymous
- "Skyscraper" by Dennis Lee
- "Bedtime Story" by Lillian Moore
- "Some Things That Easter Brings" by Elsie Parrish
- "When All the World's Asleep" by Anita E. Posey
- "Ears Hear" by Lucia Hymes and James L. Hymes, Jr.

I have also found many good, short descriptive poems in *The Random House Book of Poetry for Children* (1983). It has quite a few poems that can be used for older students (third and fourth graders) as well.

- Help students memorize the poems.

- Prepare a Poetry Book for the visualization lesson. Write one line of the poem on each of several sheets of white paper. Use 9-inch by 12-inch construction paper or blank copy paper. Prepare two 9-inch by 12-inch sheets of colored construction paper to be used later for the cover. (The book will last longer if you laminate this colored paper cover.)

An example of an illustrated student Poetry Book

Visualization and Grounding

- When you are ready to do this exercise, read through the poem with your students. Let them recite along with you.

- Then read just one line at a time and ask the children to shut their eyes to see a picture after each line. This is the key step in developing the mind's eye and ensuring that each child is participating. Always use this pause to direct all students to get a picture. Ask what each sees and let several answer. Accept differences in images.

- After one line has been read and visualized, give the sheet to a child who volunteers to draw the illustration for that line. Have that child go to work immediately before the image fades.

- With the remaining children, repeat this complete visualization process with each line or page of the poem, until you run out of pages.

- When students are finished illustrating, collect the pages and staple them between the colored covers. Put the title of the poem on the cover, and list all of the illustrators. Option: Invite the students to help put the poem in order (sequencing).

Sharing

Read the Poetry Book to the students, and allow them to read it to each other.

Evaluation

Listen to see if students can read the poem, tracking each word as they read.

Variations

1. Before the lesson, duplicate several copies of the Poetry Book, so that all children will get to illustrate the poem. This produces several illustrated copies of the same class book of poems.

2. Provide each student with all of the pages needed to illustrate the poem. Visualize the first page together as a class, then provide drawing time for everyone. Then visualize the next page together, and so on. Setting aside time for visualizing each page provides the vital step that is missing in most teaching methods. Although some students visualize without your assistance, this brief moment will ensure success for those who don't.

   This option should be extended over several days and makes a good end-of-the-day activity.

3. For second and third graders, let them do their own printing as well as illustrating, still using one line per page.

10
Enrich Oral Reading

Description

Read to students for 15–20 minutes daily. Choose selections that are interesting, high quality, and a bit above the reading level of most of the class.

Materials Needed

For the teacher:

✎ A good book

Scheduling

➤ **Every day of the school year:** For every grade, from 20–30 minutes, even more in first and second grades.

Purpose

Oral reading is a natural partner to visualization. When students are being read to, if they are not visualizing, they are not really listening and comprehending. If your students are learning improved visualization skills, then their enjoyment of oral reading should greatly increase as well.

There are many valid reasons for reading daily to your class. Among the benefits are:

• Increased vocabulary through meaningful, contextual exposure to new words.

• Appreciation of good literature.

• Opportunity to introduce students to new authors, that they might never pick independently.

- Further chances for students to practice visualization while they listen.

- A reinforcement of the value of reading by the importance it is given in the school day.

- A wealth of common stories you can use with your class for discussion, writing exercises, and higher levels of questions.

- Pure enjoyment by class and teacher alike.

Rationale

Support and validation for oral reading to students can be found in educational research. In various studies we can also find increases in visual decoding, motor encoding, and reading comprehension. These results are found in classrooms where students are read to regularly.

At the junior high and high school levels, oral reading can help fulfill requirements set by the school or the state Department of Education regarding books that all students must read at various grade levels. Oral reading of classics may take the pain and frustration out of trying to force poorer readers through a book that gives them great difficulty and little pleasure. After all, it is unlikely that students' hunger for reading and literature will be increased by forcing them through weeks of tortuous struggle.

Instead, you can read at any pace you like with your whole class, adding visualization exercises, writing assignments, and vocabulary development lessons as you go. Your whole class can acquire a common background in some classic literature. Not all of your oral reading should be of this genre, however. At the beginning of the year especially, students need to be read lighter material so they can become accustomed to listening for increasing periods of time. They need encouragement to visualize so that your words come to life as they listen.

You do not always have to do the reading yourself. Variety in oral input is enriching for the students. Here are some suggestions:

Alternatives to Reading Aloud

- Trade with another teacher. Find a teacher who is an effective oral reader, and chances are excellent that he or she will be eager to trade classes for 20 minutes a day, while you share some of your unique and special talents with the other class.

- Tell stories. The art of storytelling extends far beyond that of written literature. Storytelling has been with us since the beginning of human-kind. It is an art and a delight, and well worth the effort of sharpening your skills and learning good stories. Myths and fairytales lend themselves particularly well to this delivery style. Storytelling can also be a way to share the plots of books and plays that are beyond the reading comprehension level of your class. The stories of Shakespeare can be told at grade levels far lower than can read his works. Don't neglect the funny story. And if you have some really exciting true stories of your adventures, this is an appropriate time for them.

- Instead of reading, play recorded instrumental music of high quality. Students can shut their eyes and see whatever appears in their imaginations, and then ground by writing or drawing when the music is over. Or, you might encourage students to draw while they listen.

- Radio plays. Many radio stations broadcast old radio plays on a regular basis. *The Lone Ranger*, *The Shadow*, and *The Green Hornet* are among the old favorites once again on the airwaves. Students can visualize during the play, and then you might ask them to draw the setting or the characters, or to write a detailed description of them. Or turn the story into comic book form. The taping of these programs for personal use is permitted as long as the tape is not duplicated or distributed.

- Prerecorded literature. There are many recordings of excellent actors and actresses reading good literature.

- "Selling" books. Occasionally, do not read a whole book. Read just a chapter or two, enough to capture the students' interest. Then ask who would like to finish the story during silent reading time. This is a great way to get some new books circulating in your class.

- Capitalize on a book. After your whole class has listened to a good book, you may sometimes choose to use the book as the basis for work on comprehension skills and writing skills. For example, students can analyze plot and character, sequence the important events of the story, examine the elements of a good plot, or write opinions about what was expressed by the author. Plays and skits can center around scenes from the book.

Grounding and Sharing

If all you do is remind students to visualize as they listen, many will do so. If you also add a grounding exercise, however, participation will be much more complete and meaningful. It isn't the product that results from the grounding that imparts the value, but rather the process of students knowing that they will be representing their visual images, that encourages them to work on their clarity and creativity. Here are some grounding and sharing suggestions to pair with oral reading experiences.

- Pause the oral input from time to time and ask students to close their eyes and see what is happening, pressing for details of colors, shapes, sizes, and action. At the end of the oral input, ask students to draw a picture of their favorite scene.

- After reading the description of a character, stop and ask students to visualize this character fully. Ask questions about hair color, eye color, clothing, shoes, and height, beyond the information in the text. At the end of the day's reading, have students either draw or fully describe in writing the character that they saw in their mind's eye. Students might then pair up to compare their images.

- If your oral input describes something like an invention, a vehicle, or an unusual article of clothing, press for visualization and details. Then have students draw the object, using words to label the elements. These pictures may be displayed on a bulletin board for sharing.

- If the story comes to a point of decision, stop and give students a minute to imagine what the decision is and how its consequences unfold. Have them write their version and then read the original ending. Discuss preferences, and read some of the students' work aloud.

Note: Each of these activities is something that many teachers frequently do; the difference is that before students are asked to do them, they can be given a moment to visualize. It is this time for creative incubation that adds life to the exercise. Good visualizers visualize automatically; we need to teach the other students to do it, too.

11

Read, Write, and Respond

Description

The class reads a selection aloud together. As each section is read, quiz students about the pictures they are creating to give life to the story. Students respond to each question first in writing, then in class discussion, to increase their comprehension.

Materials Needed

For each student:

- ✎ A good short story or nonfiction article. Science magazines and articles about nature are especially good resources for this activity, or even a social studies or science textbook.
- ✎ 5-inch by 8-inch index card
- ✎ Sheet of lined paper

For the teacher:

- ✎ A list of questions you have developed about the story or article you read. Your questions should require students to answer beyond literal recall, prompting them to visualize in order to answer.

Scheduling

➤ **At any time after students are reading and visualizing:** About 30 minutes whenever you wish to increase comprehension of nonfiction (or fiction) and boost visualization skills at all grade levels.

Purpose

This type of exercise can extend the skills of visualization to nonfiction reading. Each student has time to visualize and respond independently, and then to share ideas with others. This exercise is one that actually should become part of your routine whenever your class reads together, as it deeply enriches class discussions of stories or nonfiction. It works very well in helping students comprehend their social studies textbooks, which tend to be difficult reading for most students.

Rationale

Students need to make a strong and permanent connection between visualizing and decoding. In chapter 7, page 70, when guided, they learned to link the two skills. Now, they must make the link independently. This is accomplished by lengthening the time periods between which you question each student. Every few paragraphs, interrupt the story with questions about the details of the students' own personal pictures.

In previous chapters, you planted in your poorer readers the expectation that you will call on them and expect them to have a good answer. It is important that you continue to call on all students and probe in a positive way until each student visualizes regularly from print.

Preparation

- Prepare a copy of the reading material for each student.

- Tell students that they will read together. They will use index cards to cover all but one paragraph at a time, in the way they have done before. Remind them not to read ahead.

- Tell them that they will be asked for answers to the kinds of questions that are not found in the text and will need to visualize in order to answer.

- Remind students that there are many right answers to the questions you will ask.

- Distribute text, cards, and lined paper. Have students number their papers for as many questions as you intend to ask.

Visualization

Call on various students to read as the rest of the class follows along, using the 5-inch by 8-inch index cards to keep from reading ahead.

Every few paragraphs, interrupt the story to ask for details of each student's visualization. Use the kinds of questions you have asked previously.

After asking each question, have students write their answers on paper. Then immediately discuss those answers. For complex scientific descriptions, you may need to stop and have your students draw their perceptions several times during the reading. Be sure to call on your slower readers at least as often as your top readers.

Read another paragraph or two, ask a question, record, discuss, and continue. During the discussion, if a particular student has no picture, have all the students shut their eyes while the material is reread by you or a student. To involve every student in the visualization process, do not call on anyone until you have given everyone time to think of an answer. Each student will be reviewing the visualization, building on it, and expecting to be called upon.

Sharing

This is accomplished during the class discussion. Sometimes, you might like to have students share their responses with a partner instead of with the whole class.

Evaluation

Remember that the main point of these exercises is to guide your students to create from the printed word a picture in their minds' eyes. Students' mental pictures will grow more and more accurate as they become practiced in visualizing their reading material. As a result, their comprehension and understanding usually increases markedly. You can continue to base grades on full participation on the written responses.

12
Imagery Poetry

Description

Students listen to one of a series of descriptive poems every day and respond by drawing the picture they saw while you were reading the poem aloud.

Materials Needed

For each student:

- ✎ Crayons or felt-tipped pens
- ✎ Poem Book (see Preparation)

For the teacher:

- ✎ Five fairly short descriptive poems of excellent quality, preferably non-rhyming

Scheduling

➤ **At any time after students are reading and visualizing:** 15–20 minutes a day for five days (one week) at all grade levels.

Purpose

Students tend to love funny poems and rhyming poems, but they often resist the more lyric and non-rhyming poems. This is one of the best ways I have discovered to help students at every grade level enter fully into the poet's world without resistance. For primary students, these poems are yet another path to learning beginning reading skills and strategies.

Rationale

By this time in the program, students are accustomed to visualizing, and so they do not think anything of yet another Journey. They don't even realize that they are deeply involved with genuine poetry until their mental journeys have captured their imaginations. The heart of poetry is for the poet to try to use words that will enable the reader to re-create the poet's original feelings and visions. Visualization is the perfect vehicle for leading students into a full appreciation of the poet's art.

Preparation

Before the lesson:

- Select five descriptive, engaging poems that you respond to, and whose subject matter will be interesting to your students. They could have rhymes, but this is a great exercise to introduce students to non-rhyming poetry. A good example of this kind of poem is "The Tortoise" by Byrd Baylor, which can be found in *The Random House Book of Poetry for Children* (1983).

- Type each of these poems on one portion of a separate sheet of 8½-inch by 11-inch copy paper. I like to put each poem on a different spot on each page (at the bottom of one page, along the side of another, and so on, for visual variety).

- Duplicate this set of five poem pages for all of your students. You could staple the pages together for younger students. For older students I prefer to hand out one new poem each day of the week so they don't read ahead and spoil the freshness of each day's experience.

Here are some poems I have had success with at primary levels:

- "How Do You Like to Go up in a Swing" and "Where Go the Boats?" both by Robert Louis Stevenson, from *A Child's Garden of Verses* by Robert Louis Stevenson
- "Keziah" by Gwendolyn Brooks and "The Swallow" by Ogden Nash, from *Read-Aloud Rhymes for the Very Young*, selected by Jack Prelutsky
- "The Muddy Puddle" by Dennis Lee
- "Rhyme" by Elizabeth Coatsworth
- "The Desert Tortoise" by Byrd Baylor
- "Lion" by William Jay Smith

These can be found in *The Random House Book of Poetry for Children* (1983), selected by Jack Prelutsky.

For city children, try:

- "Rainy Nights" by Irene Thompson
- "City Lights" by Rachel Field

These poems can be found in *The Random House Book of Poetry for Children* (1983).

Here are some suggestions for older students. You might also look in your grade-level literature-based reading books and your social science textbooks for more.

The following poems for older students are all to be found in *Favorite Poems Old and New* (1957):

- "This Is My Rock" by David McCord
- "Fog" by Carl Sandburg
- "City Lights" by Rachel Field
- "The Night Will Never Stay" by Eleanor Farjeon

Here are a few more, to be found in various anthologies:

- "The Surfer" by Lillian Morrison
- "Primer Lesson" by Carl Sandburg
- "Mountain Wind" by Barbara Kunz Loots
- "River Winding" by Charlotte Zolotow
- "This Is Just to Say" by William Carlos Williams

Starting the Lesson

- Pass out the Poem Books and the crayons or felt-tipped pens. Have students open their books to the first blank page, and then tell them to set aside the art materials and get ready to listen and visualize. Tell students that, when the poem has been read to them, they will be drawing one of the many pictures they will create with their minds' eyes.

- Lead the students into a relaxed mood with some stretching or slow breathing exercises.

Relaxation

You could use one of the relaxation exercises from the appendix, page 144.

Visualization: Day 1

Read the poem slowly to the students, with emphasis and feeling. (You might want to play some baroque music at the beginning of the relaxation time and continue playing the music softly as you read.)

Briefly explain any words that the students might not be familiar with, and then read the poem again. Encourage students to close their eyes; offer the blindfolds as an option to any who wish to use them.

Grounding

Have students immediately draw one of the pictures they saw. Do not allow talking until the drawing is well underway. Encourage detailed pictures.

After a few minutes of drawing, read the poem again while students continue to draw. Then instruct students to write the title and author of the poem on the blank page facing the illustration.

Sharing

Let students each sit with a partner and look at each other's pictures while the teacher reads the poem aloud again. Then ask students to briefly talk to their partners about the details in their pictures.

Visualization: Day 2

For primary: Ask students to point to words on yesterday's page as you read the poem everyone illustrated on the previous day.

For all: Beginning with some brief relaxation, repeat the routine from the first day, substituting the next poem in the Poem Book.

Visualization: Each Day Thereafter

For primary: As reading practice, students begin by reading aloud with you all of the poems that have already been illustrated. By rereading each day, many students will learn to read the poems independently. Be sure the class is tracking by following the words on the pages along with you.

For all: Follow the regular routine for illustrating the next page and sharing.

Sharing

For primary: When the book is complete, invite students to pair up with a partner and read one of their poems to each other. Have both students sign the back of the pages that they read. Then they should find a new partner and read a different poem, sign, and move on to another partner. Repeat this for about 20 minutes. Some students will read all of their poems once and then read some twice before time is up. This provides students with plenty of reading practice.

For primary homework: Have students read this book to their parents.

For older students: Because older students tend to be shy about sharing their drawings in a one-to-one situation, I wouldn't use the primary format. Instead, just discuss each day what students saw during each poem's visualization, inviting students who wish to do so to share their pictures. At the end of the week, you could invite students to donate their best picture to a bulletin board display and staple the rest together to send home.

Evaluation

For primary: Listen in when they read their poems to each other to see if they are able to read them.

For older students: Pay attention to the feeling tone in the room; are students really enjoying these poems because of the visualizations, as was your goal?

13

Vocabulary Development

Description

Choose five related words that students are not likely to know. They will image one word a day and draw what they visualize. At week's end, they will write one sentence, correctly using all the vocabulary words. To give you a model for this process, I have included a sample based on an Egyptian unit of study, using the words *delta, inundate, obelisk, papyrus,* and *scarab*. It is just a sample; you will have to create your own visualizations for the vocabulary you wish to teach.

Materials Needed

For each student:

✎ A small Vocabulary Book made just like the Memory Book, page 5.

Scheduling

➤ **At any time after students are reading and visualizing:** 20 minutes every day for one week and 10 extra minutes on Friday as often as every week, or just a few times in the school year.

Purpose

This exercise uses visualization to help students develop the skill of guessing the meaning of a new word through visualizing the surrounding material (context clues expanded with mind power). Students also learn five new words each week and share them with their parents.

Rationale

We do not increase vocabularies merely by memorizing lists of words and their meanings. To become familiar with a word, it must be experienced. Both pleasure and meaning help us to remember an incident or a word. Because these Vocabulary Books present words through pleasant, meaningful experiences, and because they keep the words in the students' attention for a span of time, the words are more likely to be retained.

By visualizing unfamiliar words, students will be more likely to image a meaning that will make sense within the sentence where they see it. This is the essence of the powerful skill of using context clues to determine word meanings. By encouraging imagination in each encounter with a new word, we train students to use context clues effectively.

Preparation

- Select five related vocabulary words that most of your students are unlikely to know well. You might find them in your social studies or science textbooks, or in your literature selections. It is often good practice to introduce students to new vocabulary *before* reading material that contains it.

- Write out five visualizations that incorporate the five new words, one for each day of the week. Each visualization should be a paragraph or two. It should include some directed scenery, building up to the introduction of the unfamiliar word and giving clues to its meaning.

- Create Vocabulary Books, just like the Memory Books, page 5.

- Have students write "Vocabulary Book" and their names on the first white page of the booklet, then number the pages 1 through 11.

- Explain to students that they will be working with their books for a week, adding one word each day. You will ask them to visualize words that they probably will not know, and to create a vivid mental picture for each word.

- Just before the start of the lesson, have students turn to page 1 in their personal Vocabulary Book and tell them that after today's Journey they will be drawing on this page the mental image they get for today's word.

Relaxation

Use any form of relaxation that you wish from the appendix, page 144. Because these visualizations are brief, you might like to try one of the longer relaxation exercises for variety.

Day One (Vocabulary Word: delta)

This is a sample for a set of words about Egypt for a social studies unit. Use it as a model for visualizations.

Sample Visualization

Read a paragraph or two to give students the context for guessing the new vocabulary word:

Today we are going to a land that is all the way on the other side of the world. It is a land of desert and sand. Imagine that you are flying over this desert, and all you can see in every direction is sand. . . . .sand dunes. . . . .sand piling up in hills and valleys. . . . . and then you notice a huge pyramid of gleaming white stone, reaching up to the sky. . . . .Next to this huge pyramid is another, nearly as big, and a third one just a little bit smaller. . . . .The sky is blue, the sun is hot, and the pyramids are shining in the sun. . . . . As you look more closely, you can see a gold tip on each white pyramid, reflecting the sun's rays. . . . .

Now you notice a wide, deep river flowing across the desert and toward the ocean. It is so wide that boats are needed to ferry people from one side to the other. From your view up in the sky you can see the river flowing from behind the pyramids, from behind the sand dunes, getting wider and wider, and more and more brown with muddy silt as it moves toward the ocean. . . . . .

*Just as the river is about to empty into the great, broad ocean, you see that something is in its way; it can't go straight ahead any more because there is a **DELTA** in its way. . . . .Take a good look at this **DELTA** . . . . . What is it made of? . . . . What shape is it? . . . . . Is there anything on it, or is it empty? . . . . . How does the river get around it, or over it, to reach the ocean? . . . .*

Grounding

Open your eyes and on page 1 write the word of the day at the top of the page.
(You should write the word on the board now, so that students spell it correctly.)
Now draw or describe in writing the delta *that you saw in your mind's eye.*
You can use words or pictures or both.

Sharing

Share by asking for volunteers to show what they drew and what they think a delta is. You may want to ask students for a show of hands to see how many had the same idea as at least a few of their classmates. Some may think it is an island, some a boat, or something else.

See if the class can come to a consensus on the true meaning of *delta.* At the end of the discussion, ask a student to find and read the definition in the dictionary. By this time, students are very eager to see who is right.

When everyone has discovered the true meaning of *delta,* have all the students either draw or write this meaning on page 2, which faces their earlier drawing. Do not allow dictionaries to be open for copying at this time; students should use their own words.

Day Two (Vocabulary Word: inundate)

Preparation

- Have a script ready for the next word. It helps students retain each of these words if each day you include the previous days' words in the visualization.

- Ask students to turn to page 3 in their Vocabulary Books.

Relaxation

Your choice.

Sample Visualization

Read a paragraph or two to give students the context for guessing the new vocabulary word.

Today let's return to the land we visited yesterday. . . . . Imagine that you are flying effortlessly over the enormous desert of sand and dunes and gleaming pyramids. . . . . .There is the river Nile that you saw yesterday, flowing past the sand, past the pyramids, past the rich, wide delta. . . . .and the river empties into the ocean, spilling its brown, muddy silt into the blues and greens of the sea. . . . .

Notice how all along the riverbank are farmlands, all very flat and empty, ready to be planted with this year's seeds. No one is on this farmland, and there are no houses or animals. . . . .the farmland is empty, waiting for the rain that is about to fall. . . . .As you watch, the clouds grow darker and darker and the rain falls. . . . .and falls. . . . .and falls . . . .

*You watch the rain fill the river, and run off the farmland into the river, until the river becomes so full of water that it begins to **INUNDATE** the land. . . . As you watch from your safe little bubble in the sky, the river **INUNDATES** the land close to it, and then it **INUNDATES** even the land farther away. . . . . .It **INUNDATES** all of the land on both sides of the river. . . . .and it **INUNDATES** the entire delta. . . . .Then the sun comes out, and slowly, slowly, not in just one day, but over several sunrises and sunsets, the **INUNDATION** recedes and the river is back to normal once more. . . . .*

Grounding

Now please turn to page 3 in your Vocabulary Books and draw or write to describe the pictures you saw about the meaning of today's word inundate. *You may use words or pictures, or both.*

Sharing

As before.

Day Three (Vocabulary Word: obelisk)

Preparation

- Have ready your visualization for today's word.

- Have students turn to page 5 in the Vocabulary Books.

 Sample Visualization

Read a paragraph or two to give students the context for guessing the new vocabulary word.

Once more we return to the land of pyramids and desert sand and the river Nile. . . . .Today you are going to land on a dirt road that leads away from the pyramids and along the edge of the river Nile. You walk along the edge of the delta, where the water inundated the land only a few weeks ago. . . . . . You can see the first green shoots of this year's planting beginning to pop up from everywhere the farmers planted them as soon as their farmland dried out from the rains. . . . . .

As you walk along, with the sun shining on the new green plants, you notice that many other people are walking along the road, too, some going the same way, some coming back. . . . .and up ahead you can see buildings with people coming out and going in. . . . . The people are not dressed in their farm clothes, but in fine white linen. . . . They are wearing their best sandals and jewelry. . . .

*You are just about to ask someone what is happening when suddenly you turn a corner and see the biggest **OBELISK** that you have ever seen, right in the middle of the road. You know that you can't climb over this **OBELISK,** because it is much too tall. . . . . .but you notice that you can get around it on either side. . . . . Stop and take a good look at this **OBELISK.** . . . . What is it made of? . . . . .How big is it? . . . . .What shape is it? . . . . . Is there anything on this **OBELISK?** . . . . .Why is it standing here in the middle of the road? . . . .*

Grounding

Now draw or describe the obelisk *from your mind's eye on page 5 in your book. You may use words or pictures, or both to describe it.*

Sharing

As before.

Day Four (Vocabulary Word: papyrus)

Preparation

- Have ready your visualization for today's word.

- Have students turn to page 7 in the Vocabulary Books.

Sample Visualization

Read a paragraph or two to give students the context for guessing the new vocabulary word. Notice the repetition of the previous day's words to optimize retention.

Let's return again to the land of the river Nile, and once more go walking on the path that leads to the obelisk. . . . .Several months have passed, and you walk past the delta and the farmlands, now with their crops growing waist high and waving in the soft Egyptian breeze. . . . .You can see from the health of the plants that the spring inundation of water from the Nile brought plenty of silt this year to enrich the land. . . .

As you walk along the path toward the obelisk, you notice a small, narrow path between the growing plants, and you follow it down to the edge of the water. You know enough not to go into the Nile, because there are crocodiles living there. . . . .They are napping now, but a splash could wake them up very quickly. . . . .Instead of going into the water, you watch the workers as they pull **PAPYRUS** *out of the water. Watch as they slice the* **PAPYRUS** *into pieces as long as their arms, and tie it in bundles for carrying back to the main road. . . . You know that the bundles of* **PAPYRUS** *are being taken to the temple where the scribes will turn them into something that they use every day. . . . .Watch as the* **PAPYRUS** *is taken into the temple and turned into this useful object. . . . . . Watch it dry in the sun until it can be used by the scribes. . . . . .*

Grounding

As before, using page 7 in the Vocabulary Books.

Sharing

As before.

Day Five (Vocabulary Word: scarab)

Preparation

- Write out your visualization for today's word. Again, try to include the previous days' words for retention.

- Have students turn to page 9 in the Vocabulary Books.

Relaxation

Your choice.

 ## Sample Visualization

Read a paragraph or two to give students the context for guessing the new vocabulary word. Notice the repetition of the previous day's words to optimize retention.

This is our last day in Egypt. . . . .our last day to walk by the delta where the spring inundation from the river Nile gave the flax and papyrus plants the rich silty soil they needed to grow tall and green. . . . .Our last day to visit the obelisk that stands by the temple where the scribes sit in the shade, writing their hieroglyphics on the fresh new sheets of papyrus. . . . .

*Today, as you walk along the path toward the temple, your eye is caught by something dark moving along beside the path. . . . .You stop to take a look, but at first all you can see is a ball of mud, about the size of a golf ball. . . . .It seems to be moving. . . . .it is moving, very slowly but steadily. . . . .You look to see what could be causing this ball of mud to roll slowly up the ground beside your path. . . . .and there it is—a **SCARAB**. . . . .Take a moment to examine this **SCARAB**. . . . . Is it alive?. . . . .Is it moving?. . . . .What color is it?. . . . .How many legs does it have?. . . . . How big is it?. . . . . .You have never seen a live one before, but now you remember that you have seen small **SCARABS** made of deep blue or green stones hanging on necklaces of the women of this country, and you have seen drawings of **SCARABS** inscribed on papyrus or even chiseled onto obelisks. . . . .You watch this **SCARAB** as it rolls the ball of mud in front of it, along the path, and you wonder what it is doing with this mud. . . . .*

Grounding

As before, using page 9 in the Vocabulary Books.

Sharing

As before. With this and all words, other concepts may come up from the visualization Journey that will help students understand more fully. Let your discussion go into other questions that students may have, and these might lead to research.

Evaluation

On the last day, after the final visualization, ask students to turn to the last page in their books, page 11. Challenge them to create a single sentence that correctly uses every word studied in this Vocabulary Book, underlining all of the vocabulary words. After all students do this, some may wish to read their sentences aloud.

Suggestions for Other Vocabulary Books

This is an excellent exercise to do on a regular basis. I like to do it about every other week, so students don't get tired of it but still get lots of practice with new words.

It is even more meaningful if you tie this activity in with your other studies. You might select words from your social studies or science units, or you might find words that will be encountered in an upcoming literature selection. Here are some suggestions just to get you thinking:

Building
architect, parapet, girder, inaccessible, grandiose, design, cantilever, skyscraper, condominium, facade, blueprint, balcony, columns

Caves
stalactite, stalagmite, spelunker, devoid of light, fissure, chasm, grotto, cavern, soluble rock, expedition, labyrinth

Circus
barker, carousel, highwire act, sideshows, exhibition, ringmaster, ferocious, outlandish, venomous, exotic, roustabouts, prestidigitator

Deserts
erosion, mesa, desiccation, drought, arroyo, flash flood, barren land, tenacious plant life, sidewinder, prospector, cantankerous

Hiking
knapsack, pitons, wilderness, rivulets, topographic map, foray, grueling climb, hazardous, provisions, ascent, monumental, buttes

Jungle
safari, expedition, explorer, profusion, flora and fauna, intrepid, ornithologist, amphibian, carnivore, herbivore

Old Ships
cargo, voyage, sheepshank, poop deck, bow, stern, starboard, keel, astrolabe, sextant, figurehead

Space
horizon, trajectory, orbit, eclipse, contraption, experimental, spacecraft, communication, device, calculation, atmosphere, acceleration

Trains
trestle, railroad ties, caboose, conductor, schedule, hoboes, highballing, freight, transport, express diner, hopper, tank car

14
Retell a Story

Description

Students will create a class book based on a traditional story such as "Three Billy Goats Gruff." Students retell the story in their own words, each student illustrates one page, and then the story is sequenced and bound. Older students read and share the story with a younger grade.

Scheduling

➤ **At any time after students are reading and visualizing:** Two sessions of 30–40 minutes at all grade levels; the lesson can be done in one day or divided over two days.

Purpose

For primary, this is yet another way to help students learn to read at the beginning levels. For older students, it provides another pathway to help students, especially lower readers, develop mental images of literature in order to increase comprehension and reading enjoyment.

Rationale

This kind of exercise is especially helpful to lower readers, because the story is so familiar that it is easy to get clear mental images. These familiar stories help students get used to visualizing while they read. Older students can be motivated to do this exercise by assigning the creation of a storybook for children at a lower grade level. After students (either a group of your lower readers or the entire class) create the book, they can visit a primary class, read the book to those students, and make a gift to the class library of the student-made book.

Chapter 14

Preparation

Before the lesson:

- Select a traditional story that you know the children will enjoy, such as "The Three Billy Goats Gruff" or "Beauty and the Beast." Primary students especially enjoy retelling a new Disney movie plot.

- The day before this lesson, read or tell the story from memory. Stop from time to time and ask students to share their visualizations about the characters, the settings, and the action.

Visualization and Grounding

- Tell students that they will be creating a class book. For older students, tell them that they will be giving it to a primary classroom and reading it to the younger students.

- Ask students to raise their hands to tell you one thing that happened in the story you read the day before. As soon as someone comes up with an event, hand him or her a sentence strip with directions to write that one event on the strip.

- Ask for another event, hand out another strip, and so on until all students have a strip to write a story element on.

- Ask students to check each other's spelling and raise their hands for your help if they are not sure. Since this book will be published, it is important that the text be properly spelled. One way to do this is to have every student ask three others to check their spelling and initial the back of the sentence strip if they agree that everything is correct.

- When all strips are complete, ask who has the first thing that happens in the story. Ask that student to read the strip aloud, and have the class vote on whether that is indeed the first thing. If the answer is yes, either have the child come to the front of the room with the strip or post the strip on a bulletin board.

- Ask who has the next element, voting by "thumbs up" or "thumbs down" on whether it really is next, and add it to the lineup of students or sentence strips. Continue in this way until all strips are in order. At this time add any essential missing parts to the story line.

  Optional: Break for the day and finish tomorrow (allowing you to double-check spelling and punctuation).

- Read the strips one at a time, asking students to visualize and inviting several students to share their mental images with the class. After each strip, ask a student who has shared some vivid images to illustrate that sentence strip. (The student pastes the strip on the bottom of a sheet of art paper and then uses the art paper for illustration.)

- Collect all the pages and mount them between two laminated sheets of colored paper. Write the title and "Illustrated by Ms./Mr./Mrs._____'s class" on the cover. (Sharpie pens will write on plastic.)

Sharing

If you teach a primary grade, read the book to the class and add it to your own library or, if you teach an older grade, take it to a primary classroom. Let students read the book and give it to the primary class as a present.

Evaluation

Each student should illustrate one page. Primary students should all be able to read the page that they wrote, and many should be able to read the whole story. Older students should be able to read the whole story aloud to younger students after some practice and assistance where needed.

Section III

Writing with the Mind's Eye

In my own classroom and also while observing lessons by my peers, I have often watched students who have been given a writing assignment. Some go to work almost right away. But many, frequently the majority, sit and fidget and stare at their pencils, apparently wondering where on earth they are supposed to find the words to put on their papers. "I don't know how to write about _____" (fill in the blank with whatever you have assigned), is the cry that goes up all over the room.

Through my experiences in teaching visualization, I have come to understand that the main problem students face in trying to write is that they have not first developed their ideas; there is no picture in their heads. Teachers try to address this problem with prewriting activities. Brainstorming, outlining, suggesting possible starts and finishes, and answering questions about the story in process are a few of the methods currently in use. All of these strategies have their benefits, but I find that for most writing assignments students merely need a few moments to shut their eyes and imagine what they want to have happen. I began teaching visualization to improve reading, but I soon realized that an unexpected side benefit was an exponential increase in the quality and fluency of my students' creative writing. If the ideas come first, and the "plot" is already clear in their minds' eyes, children are eager to begin writing. They can put their thoughts down on paper. They write in order to communicate their thoughts.

The activities in these chapters are designed to give students practice in using their minds' eyes before they write. The exercises also enable you to observe how helpful the mind's-eye moment is in many classroom writing assignments. The chapters that follow provide a jumping-off place for your imagination and artistry in the creation of effective and stimulating writing lessons.

How to Use This Section

The activities presented here can be used in any order and as often as you wish. You can also alternate using these exercises with those found in the Reading with the Mind's Eye section, page 69. You will find that visualization will be an effective tool that significantly enriches most of the writing assignments you give your students.

15

Brainstorming

Description

When given a topic, students shut their eyes and visualize while using all their senses. From this brief imaging, they generate a list of descriptive words and phrases, which you record on a chart or word bank. Students then use this word bank in their assigned writing activity.

Materials Needed

For each student:

- ✎ Writing and art paper
- ✎ Crayons or felt-tipped pens
- ✎ Piece of chalk or a white crayon
- ✎ Blindfold (optional)

For the teacher:

- ✎ Chart paper
- ✎ Felt-tipped pens of different colors

Scheduling

➤ **Any time after students are visualizing:** 30–40 minutes at all grade levels.

Purpose

Adding visualization to brainstorming increases the richness of the images and the vocabulary needed to express those images so that the ensuing writing project will be more deeply descriptive.

Rationale

Brainstorming is used in many language arts exercises as a prewriting activity. In this strategy you introduce a topic and ask students to volunteer words, phrases, and ideas related to the topic. The word bank, duly recorded by you, becomes a source of language for poems and other writing projects.

As you can imagine, the richness of language in the poems and essays will be much greater than when students work independently. Also, students expand their vocabularies as they share their words with one another. Moreover, when the mind's-eye procedure is also introduced as a part of brainstorming and writing, students will become even more involved and creative.

Preparation

- For the students' writing assignment, select a topic that will coordinate with a theme you are teaching or wish to create, or choose or adapt one of the following:

  where animals live
  winter
  friends
  fish
  fall
  trees
  how you feel in an amusement park
  characteristics of a particular animal (tiger, elephant, cat, or other)

- Decide what kind of writing product you wish the children to create: an essay, a personal opinion or experience, a poem, or other writing activity.

Starting the Lesson

- If brainstorming is unfamiliar to your class, explain how each of them can profit by the ideas of the group through this simple process. Tell them that all answers are accepted, and none are ridiculed or rejected.

- Tell students the topic of their brainstorming.

- Tell them the kind of writing product they will be creating (in this example, a certain kind of poem). Do not go into detail. When students have an idea of what they will be expected to do, they are more likely to tune into the right cues during the lesson.

❧ Sample Visualization for Brainstorming: Snow

Read the following to your class:

Boys and girls, today we are working with the topic of snow. (Write "Snow" at the top or in the center of the chart paper and circle it.)

Before we begin, let's take just a minute to relax and free our minds for lots of pictures. (Distribute blindfolds if you wish, and do a few of your favorite breathing or stretching exercises.)

Now keep your eyes closed, and imagine that you are standing in some snow . . . . . . Remember a time when you have been in snow . . . Or imagine a time you have seen movies or read books about snow . . . . . Look around and see what it looks like . . . . . Is the snow falling? . . . What does it remind you of? . . . . . Is the snow on the ground? . . . . . How does it look? . . . . . Is the snow on houses? . . . . or trees? . . . . . . or cars? . . . . . How does it make you feel? . . . .

Smell the air in this snowy place . . . . . . Listen to the sound of the snow . . . . . . Is it noisy? . . . . or quiet? . . . . . . How do your fingers feel? . . . . . . Your toes? . . . . . Now take a walk through the snow and listen to the sounds . . . . . Now open your eyes (or take off your blindfolds) *and tell me some words that describe what you saw with your minds' eyes.*

- Now ask for words that describe the topic; go through all the senses and record words on the chart. (Write the words in alternate colors for ease of reading.) First ask how the snow looks on different things. When children run out of words, have them shut their eyes again briefly and look up and down, on the trees, the ground, and the houses, and think of descriptive words. When they open their eyes with more ideas, accept literal concepts like *white* and *light*, and also encourage metaphoric phrases: soft as a kiss, like a feather, and others.

- Now ask for and record words that tell how a snowy day smells. When students run out of words, have them shut their eyes again, and this time sniff and try to remember how the snow smells: fresh, clean, clear, or like ice. As you record the words on the chart, have students help you spell, which will develop their phonic skills.

- Now ask how snow sounds, and when the first ideas run out, have students shut their eyes again and listen for the sounds. When they open their eyes, they may have more words or phrases, such as *soundless, quiet, whooshy,* or *quiet as a prayer.* Record answers and have students help with spelling.

- Then have students shut their eyes, and ask how snow feels: icy, soft, cold, squishy. Record answers on the chart paper.

- If appropriate, ask how the item being brainstormed tastes. In the case of snow, this question is a good one. (With the topic of a tiger, taste might not be very helpful.)

- From these directions you will have a list that consists mostly of adjectives and descriptive phrases. For this assignment you also need some verbs, which you can list in a different column. To elicit verbs, ask the children to shut their eyes again and notice what the snow is doing: melting, falling, drifting, tumbling, slushing, and so on. Accept phrases as well as words: making me cold, beginning to melt, or covering the rooftops.

It is especially important in the primary grades to repeat and review the words as you add more. It is hard for young children to remember the words unless you reinforce with review and repetition. The list can be used for many days as a resource for writing.

What we have done here is different from the usual procedure of brainstorming in only one way: we are directing students to use their minds' eyes and all their senses. This small difference greatly increases the richness of students' responses and involves many more children in the creative process.

Grounding and Sharing

This segment might happen later or the next day. Show students how to use the brainstormed list for the writing assignment. For instance, you might assign the following form for a poem:

The topic word:	Snow
Three describing words (adjectives):	Soft, fluffy, cold
Three -ing words (gerunds):	Tumbling, drifting, covering
One phrase:	Turning the world soft
The topic word:	Snow.

This form could be used even in first grade if you list the brainstormed words according to the categories above.

Sharing

For primary: Pair your students and have them read their poems to each other. Each partner can sign the back of the other's poem, and then find a new partner to read again. Let students read with five or six partners in this way, with both partners reading and signing each other's work.

For older students: You might read the poems aloud, leaving it up to individuals to acknowledge their work after it is heard.

Evaluation

In this kind of activity, you can use the evaluation you generally use with your students' writing. The most helpful evaluation is still that which has as its purpose the diagnosis of problems and the creation of a plan to help each child succeed.

Variations

You can do each of these on a different day:

- Ask your students to use the word bank as they write about their experiences with snow. Allow children to invent spellings phonetically as necessary for words not on the chart. For sharing, students can read their writing to each other or file it in their writing folders; later their best work may be selected for revision, editing, and publication.

- Help students learn to create a poem with a different kind of structure than the example, perhaps a haiku for older students.

    Structure of haiku:

Title:	Snow
line 1 (five syllables):	soft as a whisper
line 2 (seven syllables):	swirling, side-stepping, swishing
line 3 (five syllables):	oh, my nose is cold!

- Have students create riddles that have one of the brainstormed words or phrases as an answer. For sharing, let them read their riddles to the class and elicit guesses.

- Ask students to create a story about a person or animal that has an adventure in the snow. Ask them to decide on a main character, and then shut their eyes and watch what happens to that character in the snow. Then, using the word bank to enrich their written language, the students write about this adventure.

16
Literature Extensions

Description

A quality book of children's literature is selected and read to the students. Then they are asked to use their minds' eyes to see how the story might be re-written in the same vein. After they expand upon the ideas in the story, the children convey their thoughts through illustrations and writing.

Scheduling

➤ **At any time after all students are vividly visualizing:** 30–45 minutes at all grade levels.

Purpose

Visualization can greatly improve your students' writing. These exercises are designed to stimulate students' individual imaginations so that every child has something to write about, because every child has "seen" a story unfold and now merely needs to put it down on paper.

Rationale

For children, the purpose of writing should be to express their ideas. In order to help them, we must give students ideas to think about, and then get them to express them. A wonderful source of ideas is the body of excellent children's literature that is available to us. In this body we find ideas that deal with humor, moral decisions, fears, human frailty, mythic vision, friendship, loss and separation, family values and relationships; all of these represent ideas that touch the mind and the heart. An extremely powerful way to get students thinking about these ideas is through the mind's eye.

Good authors do not write from a dry, logical outline. Listen to them as they describe their writing process and you are likely to hear, "I just go for a walk on the beach until I meet my characters in my imagination. I talk with them, ask them what is going on in their lives, and then I go home and begin to write. I never know how the story is going to end; I have to return to the beach and ask them what is happening next." Good authors don't come up with their ideas logically or by formulas; they give full vent to their creative imaginations. This is something we can teach our students to do as well. Visualization is the key.

When To Do This Lesson

Link visualization with literature and writing any time you come across a story that provides a natural opportunity for students to write the next chapter, sequence, or alternate version.

I strongly object to the popular practice of having students write new endings to stories that they have already read. This is nearly impossible, because the students have already completely visualized the ending and cannot erase it from their imaginations. Additionally, the original ending is quite probably the best possible ending, unless you have asked your students to read the work of a poor author. (The only exception I make to this objection is when my students don't like a particular ending; in that case I challenge them to write a better, more satisfactory ending.) When you do find a story with an element that begs for a next cycle, chapter, or adventure, then make use of visualization. Read or tell the story, give your students some prompts to get them started, and then allow a moment of quiet time to watch the story unfold. You will be amazed at the quality of their prose.

I have included five examples below, but you will be able to use this approach in one way or another almost any time that you ask your students to write. Only one example *(The Elephant's Child)* is for upper grades; the rest are for primary. Always give that moment of creative incubation *before* you ask students to write.

Rosie's Walk by Pat Hutchins

For grades K–1

Materials Needed

For each student:

✎ Writing and art materials

For the teacher:

✎ The book *Rosie's Walk*
✎ Chart paper and felt-tipped pens or chalk and a chalkboard to record class ideas

Preparation

- Hand out writing and art materials. Have students set them aside.

- Show the illustrations as you read the book to your class. Discuss why the fox keeps getting hurt.

 ## Visualization

Read the following to your class:

Now shut your eyes and imagine Rosie in another part of the farmyard. Imagine that she is walking along. Raise your hand when you see where she is walking. (When many students' hands are up, ask where students see her. Write down the answers. This word bank will help students when they start to write.)

Now shut your eyes again and see Rosie in the place you just told me about. Now here comes the fox. We know he is not going to catch her, but what is going to happen to him! See him trying to catch her . . . watch . . . and see what happens to him. Raise your hand when you see what happens.

Grounding

Write where Rosie was walking and what happened to the fox when he tried to catch her. If you wish, you can draw a picture to go with your writing.

Sharing

A class book of each student's illustrated text can be made, read to the class, and put into the class library.

You can also ask students to shut their eyes again and imagine another place that Rosie is walking and another misfortune that befalls the fox. If you repeat this exercise over several days, students can write and draw five or six pages and make individual books. These can be read to friends, teachers, and parents.

Evaluation

Use the evaluation procedure you normally use for your students' writing.

Imogene's Antlers by David Small

For grades K–3

Materials Needed

For each student:

✎ Writing and art materials

For the teacher:

✎ The book *Imogene's Antlers*
✎ Chart paper and felt-tipped pens or chalk and a chalkboard to record class ideas

Preparation

- Hand out writing and art materials. Have students set them aside.

- Show the illustrations from the book as you read the story to your class. Discuss the problem, how Imogene handled it, and how her mother handled it. Then do a visualization exercise.

Visualization

Read the following to your class:

Close your eyes now and see Imogene in her antlers. Notice how she is feeling with antlers on her head. See the antlers decorated with doughnuts . . . . . See them decorated like a Christmas tree . . . . . See Imogene going to bed with her antlers sticking up at the top of the bed . . . . . Now it is morning . . . . . See her appear at the kitchen door with a peacock's tail.

Now let's imagine Imogene going to bed that night . . . See her get that enormous peacock's tail into bed . . . . . . And now she goes to sleep . . . . . The next morning she wakes up . . . . . and the peacock tail is gone. Instead, Imogene has part of another animal on her. Look and see what it is . . . . . . When you see what it is, raise your hand. (Wait until most hands are up. Then ask for and write the responses on a chart or on the chalkboard.)

Now shut your eyes again and see this new animal part that Imogene woke up with. See her walk down to the kitchen and surprise her mother. Just watch Imogene for a minute and see one trouble she is going to have with this new animal part. Is there something she can't do? Or will this new part help her in some way? Watch and see . . . . . (Wait about 30 seconds for the class to see the events.)

Grounding

Ask students: *What did you see on Imogene? . . . What trouble or help was the animal part you saw? . . . Draw Imogene with the animal part, and write a sentence or more about the trouble or help that the animal part caused.*

This exercise can be repeated several times, and your students can put all their writing and pictures into an "Imogene's Antlers" book. Be sure to give the original author credit by putting his name on the book. If you ask the students each to do only one picture, their work can be bound into a class book for students to read.

Sharing

If you make a class book, read it to the students and put it in the class library.

If everyone makes an individual book, ask the students to read their books to a partner, to the teacher, and to their families as homework. Have each listener sign the back of the reader's book until each student has five or six signatures. This sharing provides practice in reading as well as writing and gives the students an immediate chance to read any phonetic spelling before they forget what they meant to say.

Evaluation

Use the evaluation procedure you normally use for your students' writing.

Cloudy with a Chance of Meatballs by Judi Barrett

For grades K–3

Materials Needed

For each student:

- ✎ Writing materials

For the teacher:

- ✎ The book *Cloudy with a Chance of Meatballs*
- ✎ Chart paper and felt-tipped pens or chalk and a chalkboard to record class ideas

Preparation

- Hand out writing materials. Have students set them aside.

- Read the story to your class and show the illustrations while you read.

Visualization

Read the following to your students:

Now close your eyes and get a picture of our own town. There is our school . . . . and there is the street out in front of the school . . . . . . Now see your own house . . . . . . and yard . . . . . and your friends' houses . . . . . . Now imagine that in our town we get something that we need from the clouds every day. Not food, as in Chewandswallow, but something else. Something we all need, raining down from the sky.

In Chewandswallow, the people needed food three times a day, but this new thing you are seeing might be needed only once a day, or once a week . . . . . See the friendly clouds . . . . They are bringing something we all need . . . . . Watch as the things begin to fall from the clouds. As soon as you see what is falling, raise your hand so I will know you are ready.

(As soon as many hands are up, ask students what they saw. List these things on chart paper or on the chalkboard. If some students didn't get an idea, they can borrow their classmates' ideas for the next part of the imaging.)

*Now shut your eyes again and see this stuff coming down from the clouds,
and the people in our town using whatever is falling from the clouds . . . . .
Watch to see what the children do . . . . . and the grownups . . . . Do any of
these things fall on the houses, or do they fall only where they are needed? . . . .
What do the people in our town do with the leftovers?*

Grounding

Tell students: *Write down what you saw in your minds' eyes. Write so clearly
that others can see the same picture that you saw.*

When you stress the need for clarity, students understand the reason for writing—
to communicate our thoughts to others.

Sharing

These stories can be bound into a class book to go in the class library, or students
can read their stories to a given number of other students, who sign their names
on the back.

Evaluation

Use the evaluation procedure you normally use for your students' writing.

The Runaway Bunny by Margaret Wise Brown

For grades K–3

Materials Needed

For each student:

- ✎ Crayons
- ✎ Pencils
- ✎ Story paper (Story paper has lines on the bottom and a big blank
  space for drawing at the top.)

For the teacher:

- ✎ The book *The Runaway Bunny*

Preparation

As you read the book to your class, show the wonderful illustrations.

 ## Visualization

Read the following to your class:

As you shut your eyes, I want you to imagine that you are the little bunny. You are sitting in the grass by your mother and you want to run away . . . . You can't run to the mountaintop because your mother will become a mountain climber and climb to where you are. You can't become a flower in a hidden garden because she will become a gardener and find you.

So you have to imagine someplace where you can try to hide from this mother of yours. Raise your hand when you see where you can go to hide. (Wait at least 30 seconds or until most hands are up. Then ask ten or more students to tell where they are going to hide.)

Now shut your eyes again and see where you are hiding . . . . Now see what the mother is going to do to find you. Raise your hand when you know. (Wait again until most hands are up.)

Grounding

If your hand is up, you may begin drawing a picture of yourself as a little bunny and your mother. Then complete the sentences that I will put on the board:

Said the little bunny, "I will be a _____."

"If you become a _____," said his mother, I will be a _____ and _____.

(This pattern follows the one used repeatedly in the book and so should be familiar and easy to use. For first graders I put the frame sentences on white paper so that each child can write in the missing parts.)

For example, one child wrote:

Said the little bunny, "I will be a piece of gold hidden in the earth."

"If you become a piece of gold hidden in the earth," said his mother, "I will be a leprechaun and find you and put you in my pot."

Sharing

Make a class book.

Evaluation

Use the evaluation procedure you normally use for your students' writing.

The Elephant's Child by Rudyard Kipling

For all grades

Materials Needed

For each student:

- ✎ Crayons
- ✎ Pencils
- ✎ Story paper

For the teacher:

- ✎ A copy of *The Elephant's Child* which is included in *Four Famous Just So Stories*

Preparation

- Hand out materials and have students set them aside.

- Read or tell the story to your class, and show the illustrations.

 Visualization

Read the following to your class:

Shut your eyes and see an animal that has an unusual part, like the long neck on a giraffe. (Allow 30 seconds or more.) *Raise your hands as soon as you can see one. Tell me the unusual part of your animal.*

(Ask eight or ten students to name the animal they saw and together identify the unusual part. Tell students who didn't see one of their own that they can pick their favorite of all these ideas.)

Now shut your eyes again and see where your animal likes to live . . . . Watch it as it plays in its own habitat . . . . Now imagine that the unusual part of the animal is missing. For instance, the giraffe now has a short little neck. The peacock has a tiny boring tail; the tiger has no stripes . . . . . (Use some of the examples that the children gave you.) See back in time . . . . See back to a time before this animal had its unusual part.

Now watch and see what adventure happens to this animal to give it its unusual thing. The adventure that gave the elephant's child his long nose was the crocodile pulling on the elephant's trunk. What kind of adventure could give your animal its unusual part? Watch and see. (Wait in silence for about one minute.)

Grounding

As soon as you know what happened to your animal, start drawing a picture of it on your story paper. Then write the words that tell what happened. If you haven't been able to see an adventure yet, raise your hand, and I will come around to help you get an exciting picture.

Circulate and ask students to tell you what the adventure was. Be sure to visit those children who often have difficulty getting started, and offer some suggestions for possible adventures. Even if you make the suggestion, have the child try to see a picture of it actually happening in his or her mind's eye.

Sharing

This exercise is a good candidate for a class book. Bind all of the students' completed sheets together in one book. Read it to the class.

Option: Have every child read his or her "story" to at least five other students who then sign the back of the reader's story paper.

Evaluation

Use the evaluation procedure you normally use for your students' writing.

Note: For years I tried to get my students from grades 1–8 to write "why" tales (how the _____ got his _____) with very little success. I finally realized that students couldn't write a story about how the tiger *got* its stripes because in their minds' eyes it already *has* stripes. Only by inviting children first to imagine the object of the story *without* its special characteristic was I able to get wonderful results.

17
Story Maps

Description

Read or tell a story where there is some movement over geography. Students then draw an overhead view of the scenery.

Materials Needed

For each student:

- 9-inch by 12-inch sheet of art paper
- Crayons or felt-tipped pens

For the teacher:

- A story with some movement through different locations, such as "Little Red Riding Hood"
- Chart paper or overhead projector
- Pens to model the process

Scheduling

➤ **At any time after students are reading and visualizing:** Two sessions of 30–40 minutes are needed to teach students how to do this exercise, depending on the length of the story that you select. After you have done this once, you could repeat it in about 30–40 minutes at any time of the year.

Purpose

This exercise helps students make sense of locational movement within a story through visualization of an overhead, topographical view.

Rationale

In many stories, especially adventures, the story takes place over a geographical area. Some books, such as *The Hobbit* by J.R.R. Tolkien, include a map to help the reader make sense of the story action. Having students create their own visual maps of the story often can aid with comprehension. It also teaches students some general mapmaking skills and concepts.

Preparation

- Review the plot of "Little Red Riding Hood" so you will be prepared to tell the story as an example.

- For future exercises: select a story where creating a map would help students understand the story action.

Visualization and Grounding

Session One

- Retell, with students' help, the story of "Little Red Riding Hood."

- With students' verbal assistance create a map of the story on a chart or overhead projector. Ask:

  What has to be on our map?
  Where should we put Little Red's house?
  What else has to be here? (forest)
  And where should we put the forest?
  What else do we need? (Grandma's house)
  Where should Grandma's house go?
  What else do we need? (a path)
  Should the path be straight? Why not? (shortcut)
  What else do we need? (The flowers Little Red stops to smell)

  Do not draw the characters, just the scenery where they will act. Your story map might look like the drawing on the following page.

- Now ask students to draw their own version of a map for "Little Red Riding Hood."

Session Two

- Read a new story ("The Three Little Pigs" would work).

- Ask students to help you list all of the elements that should be in this map.

- Then ask students to make their own versions of the map, being sure to include all of the elements.

A story map for "Little Red Riding Hood"

For Chapter Books

When you are reading a complex book where geography is a major element, such as *Island of the Blue Dolphins* by Scott O'Dell, *My Brother Sam Is Dead* by James Lincoln Collier or *Abel's Island* by William Steig, create a large class map on a bulletin board. Each day, when you read a chapter, students can help you add the elements that are revealed in that section of the story. Doing so can really help students with their comprehension of the book and provides an ongoing visual aid to help them stay involved with the story's complexity.

Sharing

Primary students might like to post their story maps on a bulletin board. One way that makes the sharing of drawings safer for older students is to ask them all to leave their papers on their desks and then walk around the room looking at other students' work. Set a ground rule of making either no comments or only positive comments.

Evaluation

As usual, evaluate for participation and ability to get a visual picture, and remediate if necessary through motivational strategies.

18

Poem Partners

(For intermediate and upper grades)

Description

Students write a poem in partnership with a well-known poet. Read one line of the poem, then have the students each write the next line. Repeat the process until the poem has been completed.

Scheduling

➤ **Any time after all students are vividly visualizing:** 20–30 minutes from grades 3 to 8.

Purpose

This activity allows students to enter into the flow of a genuine poet, learning to write poetry through acquiring an internal feel for a good poem. It helps students write poetry with the heart of a poet, for the purpose of sharing a vivid feeling or image with another human being. Many of these poems will not be rhyming, but lyric, descriptive, or in free verse—a format that many students need support and encouragement with to become comfortable.

Rationale

It is difficult to teach students of any age to write lyric poems. Although we can inspire jingles and pattern poems, such as cinquaines and diamontes, genuine poetry that paints a picture for its reader is much more difficult for children to write. When we help students create vivid mental images and then provide them with the language of a fine poet, we are giving them an excellent foundation upon which to write their own descriptive poems.

Preparation

- Find a high-quality poem, preferably a non-rhyming one, by a poet who paints a strong visual or emotional picture with words. It should be brief, not more than 10–12 lines. Here is a sample poem:

"Heart Stones" by Laura Rose

A stone, so smooth and round,
Can fill my palm with whispers of the river that shaped it
By rushing waters cold and swift.
A stone, so grand and tall
Cries challenge with a dare of, "Can you climb me?"
And now I cannot bear to stick to earth.
A stone, a tiny pebble,
Can hop in my shoe and stop me in my tracks,
Though smaller than a seed.
But if I were a stone, you would find me deep within the earth,
Below the dirt, below the rocks, shining out loud,
A diamond waiting to come awake.

Visualization and Grounding

Today you will be visualizing, then writing, then visualizing again.
You may shut your eyes, or you may find that you can get a clear picture with your eyes open. You decide.

In our Journey today, we are going to be poem partners with a famous poet.
I am going to read you a line from (tell the title and author of your selection) *and then you will write the next line. Before we start, listen to the entire poem so that you will know where it is going.*

(Read the entire poem.)

Now I'm going to read the first line only. I want you to get a clear mental image, and then write the next line to help the reader see what you are seeing. Your words do not need to rhyme, they just need to add to the clarity of the image. For instance, you might read the first line of the poem and add some descriptive words of your own. For example:

The poet writes: *A stone, so smooth and round.*
Then you might suggest: *Round as a penny, round as a plum.*

Chapter 18

Now you try it. Here's the first line (Read it.) *Your turn.* (Wait until all students have written something and then ask several to share: each time you read the poet's line, ask a student to respond with his or her line. This gives students a model for how to do this well.)

Continue this process until the poem is complete:

1. Read one of the poet's lines.

2. Ask students to write the next line.

3. Read the poet's next line.

4. Students write the next line. (Every student's poem will be different.)

Example

"Heart Stones"

A stone, so smooth and round, (original)
Round as a baseball, round as a plum (student's addition)

Can fill my palm with whispers of the river that shaped it (original)
For me to hold in my hand today (student's addition)

By rushing waters cold and swift. (original)
Cold and hard as icy fingers. (student's addition)

A stone so grand and tall (original)
Tall as a tower, grand as a mountain. (student's addition)

Cries challenge with a dare of, "Can you climb me?" (original)
"Can you reach the top—do you dare?" (student's addition)

And now I cannot bear to stick to earth. (original)
And my feet take me up the stone's face toward the sky. (student's addition)

A stone, a tiny pebble, (original)
Barely bigger than a grain of sand (student's addition)

Can hop in my shoe and stop me in my tracks, (original)
Until I stop and take off my shoe, empty my shoe (student's addition)

Though smaller than a seed. (original)
I can't believe I could even feel it! (student's addition)

But if I were a stone, you would find me deep within the earth, (original)
I'd be hiding there, unknown, unseen (student's addition)

Below the dirt, below the rocks, shining out loud, (original)
Like the sun shining in the stones (student's addition)

A diamond waiting to come awake. (original)

Final Activity

Have students write the entire poem (I like to do this as a handwriting lesson). You will want to check their spelling to ensure it is correct. Then display the original poem on the board or overhead projector with space between each line. Students copy onto good paper one line of the poem and then one of their own. Many students take this opportunity to revise their work.

Sharing

This is the most delightful part of the lesson. Students volunteer to read their poems. We can do this two ways. In the first option, I read the poet's line and the student reads the next line. Then I read the next, and the student responds. We finish the entire poem together. The second option is to let the student read his or her entire poem. I like to bring in a microphone and have the student who is partner reading use it.

You can also display all of these poems on a bulletin board. If you do four or five of them, students can select their best for the final rewrite and display.

Evaluation

Evaluate these as you would any of your students' writing.

19

Other Times to Use Visualization in Writing

I have offered you some scripted lessons to start you thinking about how visualization can be used in specific writing situations. It is my belief that nearly all creative writing experiences take a quantum leap in depth and quality when students have an opportunity for visualization.

I hope you will add visualization to just about every writing assignment. If you do not, your students' sluggish reactions to being asked to write should help you remember why visualization is very important. If, when you give the order, "Okay, start writing," several students sit with blank expressions on their faces, just staring at their pencils, this is a signal that they have not yet thought of anything to write about. It is the perfect opportunity to back up and add a moment of visualization, of picturing the characters and watching the action unfold.

In addition to reaping the benefits of improved writing content, students who visualize before they write are learning to employ an invaluable kind of thinking and creating. These skills will enrich them throughout their lives.

Conclusion

Most of our students spend precious little time in a state of creative wondering. When they have a free moment, they turn to television, Nintendo, video movies, or arcade games. Our children need to be taught to take time for their own creative thoughts. In our frenetic culture, reflection, non-convergent thought, imagining, dreaming, and visualizing are not only permissible but foundational to creative work.

It is my hope that, by reading this book and trying the exercises, you will develop a frame of mind in which you notice all the places in each day where visualization will enhance many moments of your school year.

Use visualization whenever you want your students to construct meaning in their studies. Use it when they read in any context: fiction, nonfiction, literature, social studies, science, and theater. Teach your students to use visualization when they are being read to and when they are reading quietly to themselves. Offer students a moment of silence for visualization before any writing activity, especially those exercises in which creativity is an enormous asset.

Once you become committed to the regular inclusion of visualization, you develop an attitude that helps you see the world of learning through your students' eyes. You realize that you cannot teach meaning to your students; they must find it or create it for themselves; visualization is the perfect tool to achieve this heightened creative state.

By purposefully teaching your students to visualize as they read and write, you will involve them more deeply in their studies, and you will see comprehension and personal enjoyment considerably deepen and grow.

And remember that we humans can create only what we can imagine. When you help your students learn and share through their reading what others have imagined, then the world will have its best chance to embrace wild ideas such as friendship, compassion, world peace, environmental harmony, and an end to hunger. The ideas shared in books can hold the keys to the knowledge and the imagination that will make our world work. Let's give our students the skills to unlock those gates.

Appendix: Relaxation Exercises

Note: Wherever you see this: . . . ., each dot each signifies a pause of about one second. They are just reminders to slow down. You should feel free to adjust the timing for your students. If you engage in the exercise at the same time that you are reading it, you will get the best sense of when to read each new sentence.

Tense and Relax

This exercise is written out on page 6 of chapter 1. It is one of the best: it is brief and effective and can be used repeatedly for just about any Journey.

Tensing Muscles

Be sure your feet are flat on the floor . . . . Shake out your shoulders . . . . Now put your hands on your desktop and sit with your back straight and relaxed . . . . as if your head were a round ball resting gently on a column of golden building blocks . . . Let gravity and balance, not your muscles, do the work of holding your body upright . . . . See if you notice any tense places in your body today . . . . Let them relax as much as you can . . . . Remember that we are trying to become both relaxed and alert, calm and ready.

Start today by focusing your attention on your feet. Tense every muscle in your feet. Do not tense any other part of your body if you can help it . . . . Squeeze only the muscles in your feet, tighter and tighter . . . . tighter . . . . . and tighter . . . . . and then let all the tension go . . . . Take a deep breath all the way in . . . . . and all the way out . . . .

Now try to tense only the muscles in your legs and knees and thighs, not your feet . . . Do not tense any muscles other than those in your legs and knees and thighs . . . . tighter . . . tighter . . . tighter . . . now let all that go . . . . Take a deep breath all the way in . . . and all the way out . . . . . .

Now tense your shoulders and arms and hands . . . . . tighter . . . tighter . . . tighter . . . and then let go . . . . Take a deep breath, all the way in . . . . and all the way out . . . .

Now, lastly, tense your head and neck and all the parts of your face. Your mouth, nose, forehead, cheeks, eyes, ears, everything, tense them all up tighter . . .

tighter . . . tighter . . . and tighter . . . . Now let it all go . . . . Now we will take just two more deep breaths, all the way in . . . and all the way out . . . . and all the way in . . . . and all the way out . . . . .

Tension Dial

Please put your feet flat on the floor . . . . Shake out your shoulders . . and your arms . . . . . your hands and fingers . . . . and put your hands quietly on your desktop . . . . Please pay attention to your breathing; don't change it, just notice how it is . . . . notice if you are breathing into your chest or into your stomach . . . . Are you breathing through your nose or through your mouth? . . . . Feel the air go in . . . and out . . . . .

All of us carry a certain amount of tension all of the time. In this exercise we want to lower that tension as much as we can, because it can keep our body from doing its best job for us. You have been watching and noticing your breathing; now I want you to notice the level of tension in your muscles . . . . Are they tense or relaxed? . . . . . . Maybe you have a lot of tension today . . . Sometimes, when we are worried or tired, we hold more tension than usual . . . Whatever you are feeling is just fine for you at this moment . . . Perhaps you don't feel very much tension today . . . Just notice what your level is . . . . . in your feet . . . . . your legs . . . . . your shoulders . . . . . just notice if they are tense or relaxed . . . .

I want you to call the level of tension that you have right now in your body a tension level of 5. Think of a dial that is your own tension control dial. Now it is set at 5. That is right in the middle. This dial can go up to 10 and down to 1. Right now your dial is set on 5.

Now I want you to turn the dial up to 6. . . You feel a little more tension than before . . . . . Turn it up to 7 . . . . . Up to 8 . . . . . Now let it slip back to 7 . . . . . back to 6 . . . . . back to 5 . . . . . This is where you started.

Now turn it up again, more tension . . . up to 6 . . . 7 . . . 8 . . . now up to 9 . . . . then let it slide down to 8 . . . 7 . . . 6 . . . 5 . . . down to 4 . . . . . down to 3 . . . . . Now go back up to 4 . . . . . and then to 5 . . . . Let's go up again just a little to 6 . . and 7 . . . then back down to 6 . . . 5 . . . 4 . . . 3 . . . down even more to 2 . . . . . then let it go down as far as you wish . . . . . Keeping the dial at this low level, notice your breathing now . . . See if there is any difference in how you are breathing now . . . . Now put the dial wherever you would like it to be . . . you can stay at 1 if you like, very relaxed and alert . . . . . or you can put it on another setting . . . . .

Be a Tree

Put your feet flat on the floor . . . . and shake out the tension from your shoulders and arms and hands . . . . Place your hands on your desktop . . . . Take several deep breaths . . . . all the way in . . . . and all the way out . . . . . and in . . . . feeling the oxygen traveling down to your legs and knees and toes . . . . and out . . . . . And once more all the way in, this time sending the oxygen into your throat and head and brain . . . and all the way out . . . .

Now see yourself as a tree planted firmly in a meadow . . . . You can feel your roots going deep into the earth to support you and bring you moisture . . . . . Feel the strength and support that these roots give you . . . . . You can feel your trunk, straight and strong, holding you perfectly upright, to help you stay healthy and balanced . . . Moisture flows up your trunk from your roots, life-giving water . . . . .

You can feel your branches spreading to the sun . . . . And you can feel the sun pouring its energy down on your leaves . . . . The leaves soak up the sunlight, growing warmer and full of energy from the sun . . . . Allow yourself to enjoy this feeling of being a tree . . . . . with the sun's energy coming into you from your upturned leaves and the earth's strength and energy supporting you from below . . . . . And take one more deep breath, all the way in . . . . and all the way out . . . .

Air and Space

Be sure that your feet are not crossed and are placed firmly on the floor. Shake out your shoulders and arms and hands, and then put them gently on your desktop. Remember, you are relaxing your body, but you are not trying to fall asleep. You want to be relaxed and also fully alert . . . . Take five deep breaths. (Time these to your own slow and deep breathing.) All the way in . . . . . and all the way out . . . . . (Repeat a total of five times.)

Now imagine that your body is made mostly of air and space. Imagine that you are so full of space that you are getting lighter and lighter. Your head almost floats upward instead of nodding down. You notice that your whole body is pressing less and less on the chair where you are sitting. You are growing so light that suddenly you notice that you are really beginning to float upward. You float like a balloon, up toward the ceiling . . . . . You realize that you can gently bounce all around the room, like the astronauts inside their space capsules. Your motion is slow, but you can bounce anywhere . . . . You bounce off a wall . . . .

off the ceiling . . . . off the floor . . . off the bookcase . . . Since you are made mostly of air, you don't disturb anything, but the papers do flutter as you pass by . . . .

Gently now, you will lower your spacious body slowly, slowly, down to your chair. Feel the floor beneath your feet again, and the chair underneath your body. Let your body rest comfortably, while you get ready to go on today's Journey.

Raindrops

Please put your feet flat on the floor . . . Shake out your shoulders . . . shake your arms and hands . . . now put them gently on your desktop . . . Balance your spine so that gravity is doing the work of holding your body upright . . . . Sway back and forth a little until you find that center of gravity . . . . Let your body be relaxed and alert . . . . . Now take a slow deep breath, all the way in . . . . . and all the way out . . . . . . Now imagine that you are dressed in shorts and a light top, and you are standing in warm sand on a tropical island . . . . . You can feel the warm sand on the bottoms of your bare feet and between your toes . . . . you wiggle your toes in the sand . . . . . The air around you is warm and heavy . . . . . there is no breeze at all . . . . Suddenly you hear the sound of big raindrops splattering on the leaves of the nearby trees, hitting your hair . . . . . your shoulders . . . your nose . . . . You know that there is no reason to run for cover, because the rain that comes every afternoon is always warm and pleasant, and no one cares if you get wet today . . . . So you stand there with your feet in the sand, ready to enjoy this tropical shower . . . . . As the raindrops come more quickly, you can hear them falling on the leaves of the trees . . . . . faster and faster . . . . and you feel each individual drop as it gently falls on your head . . . . and your arms . . . . You turn your face up to the sky, and the drops fall on your cheeks and chin and forehead, and on your closed eyelids . . . .

Now you turn your face back down, because the rain is heavier, still warm and gentle, but coming down in greater and greater amounts. So many raindrops are falling that the water begins to run off you in little streams. Water streams off your head, off your shoulders . . . . and down your back . . . . . You stand there, listening to the rain in the trees . . . . smelling the rain hitting the dry sand . . . . enjoying this shower of warm rain . . . .

Now the rain slows . . . . . You can feel the individual droplets again . . . . and it stops . . . . . Notice the silence . . . . . then the birds begin to sing . . . . and the sun comes out to dry the water from the trees and the sand and you . . . . . Now you leave this warm island and return to our classroom, ready for today's Journey.

Colored Air

Please be sure that your feet are flat on the floor . . . and shake out your shoulders . . . . and now put your hands gently on your desktop and sit in an upright position . . . I want you to balance your weight on your spinal column . . . Gravity and balance should do most of the work of holding your body upright so that your muscles can be relaxed and at ease . . . . You are aiming for a state that is both alert and relaxed . . . peaceful and energized . . .

Today, we are going to breathe in some colors, in long slow breaths. First, imagine that you are breathing in purple air . . . . The purple air fills your lungs and chest and then travels all the way to your fingers . . . . As you exhale, all the purple air leaves your body, back to your lungs and out of your mouth . . . . Breathe in another deep breath of purple air. It travels down your arms to your fingers and down your stomach and legs into your toes . . . . As you exhale, it all flows back into your lungs and out of your mouth.

Next, breath in some blue air . . . Slowly fill your lungs with blue air and watch it go down your arms into your fingers, and down your legs into your toes . . . . As you exhale, watch it go back up your legs into your lungs, back up your arms into your lungs, and out of your mouth into the air. Let's breathe the blue air once again . . . notice how it smells going in . . . and exhale . . . . Notice the blue air as it leaves your mouth and goes back into the room.

Now orange . . . send orange air into every part of your body—legs and feet and toes, shoulders and arms and fingers . . . then back out in an orange cloud. Now turn the cloud yellow and breathe it in . . . sending yellow to every part of your body, like sending sunshine . . . . Let it flow up your neck and into your head and brain . . . . And then exhale and let it all go back to your lungs and out of your mouth . . . .

Now just notice your normal breathing for a moment . . . .

Golden Bubbles

Please put your feet flat on the floor . . . Shake out your shoulders . . . . . your head . . . . . your arms . . . . . . your hands and fingers . . . . Now place your hands gently on your desktop . . . . . and sit up straight and relaxed.

Imagine that a string is attached to the exact center of the top of your head, and it is gently tugging your head upward into perfect balance on the top of your spinal cord . . . . . very gently tugging your head into perfect balance . . . . .

Now, in your mind's eye, take a look at your spinal column. It is made up of separate little bones that are stacked on top of each other like a very tall stack of blocks. Between each of the little blocks called vertebrae is a little cushion that keeps the bones from rubbing against each other when you move. Today we are going to imagine that each cushion is actually a small golden bubble . . . See the bones in your spinal column . . . . the vertebrae, each held apart from the next by a soft, golden bubble . . . . . . The bubbles don't force the bones apart, they cushion and protect them from each other . . . .

You can feel the golden bubbles, lifting each vertebra, adding just a tiny bit to your height as you sit in your chair . . . . . We are going to take five deep breaths now, and as we do, I would like you to imagine that some of the air you breathe is going to fill those little golden bubbles. Don't fill them too full; you don't want to make your back uncomfortable. Fill them just so they support and cushion your vertebrae like little golden pillows.

Breathe all the way in . . . and feel the golden bubbles expand gently to lift and separate each vertebra . . . . . and all the way out . . . . the bubbles get a little smaller, but they still protect each little bone . . Breathe all the way in . . . . . the golden bubbles expanding . . . . and all the way out . . . . And all the way in . . . little golden cushions all up and down your back . . . . . and all the way out . . . . and all the way in . . . golden bubbles lift each vertebra . . . and all the way out . . . . and once more, all the way in, feeling the golden bubbles gently expand . . . and all the way out . . . .

Center of Balance

Now put your feet flat on the floor . . . And shake out your shoulders and your arms and hands . . . . Put them gently on your desktop . . . Remember that you want to put yourself in a relaxed but alert state . . . You are going to search for the center of gravity of your body. I want you to sit up straight, as relaxed as you can allow your body to be . . . . . Now sway your whole body, not just your head alone, but your whole body, slightly to the left . . . then to the right . . . just slightly, go back and forth, noticing at what point you pass right through your center of gravity . . . Concentrate on that center and keep slowly swaying . . . . . a little less each time . . . . . until you come to rest right in your exact center of gravity. Here your body has to do very little work to stay upright, because you are centered in space.

Now we will do the same thing, this time moving forward and back. Sway slightly forward . . . . . and slightly back . . . . . then forward . . . . . and back . . . . . looking for the spot where you pass through the center of gravity . . . .

As you find it, make your movements smaller and smaller until you stop exactly in your own center . . . . .

Notice how easy it is to be perfectly upright when you have found this center of gravity. You can be completely relaxed while still staying completely alert and ready for anything that happens. This kind of centering of the body is what judo and karate experts use to be fully alert. When we tense our bodies to face difficulty, we only slow them down. But when the body is in this state of calm alertness, it is ready for quick movement.

Be aware again of your own center . . . . . Shift slightly back and forth and return to the center once more . . . . . Shift a little to the left . . . and right . . . and then return to center . . . . .

Now take five deep breaths. (Time these to your own slow and deep breathing.) Breathe all the way in . . . . and all the way out . . . . (Repeat a total of five times.)

Student Reading Resource List

Barrett, Judi. 1978. *Cloudy with a Chance of Meatballs.* New York: Scholastic.

Brown, Margaret Wise. 1942. *The Runaway Bunny.* New York: Harper & Row.

Collier, James Lincoln. 1974. *My Brother Sam Is Dead.* New York: Simon & Schuster Books for Young Readers.

Favorite Poems Old and New. 1957. Selected by Helen Ferris. Garden City, N.Y.: Doubleday.

Hazbry, Nancy, and Roy Condy. 1983. *How to Get Rid of Bad Dreams.* Richmond Hill, Ontario: Scholastic TAB.

Hunt, Irene. 1964. *Across Five Aprils.* New York: Temple Books.

Hutchins, Pat. 1968. *Rosie's Walk.* New York: Scholastic.

Kent, Jack. 1986. *Joey.* North Ryde, N.S.W.: Angus & Robertson.

Kipling, Rudyard. 1942. *Four Famous Just So Stories.* Garden City, N.Y.: Doubleday.

Lawson, Robert. 1939. *Ben and Me.* Boston: Little, Brown & Co.

O'Brien, Robert C. 1971. *Mrs. Frisby and the Rats of N.I.M.H.* New York: Atheneum.

O'Dell, Scott. 1967. *The Black Pearl.* Boston: Houghton Mifflin.

———. 1960. *Island of the Blue Dolphins.* Boston: Houghton Mifflin.

Ormondroyd, Edward. 1963. *Time at the Top.* London: Heinemann.

Politi, Leo. 1950. *A Boat for Peppe.* New York: Scribner.

The Random House Book of Poetry for Children. 1983. Selected and introduced by Jack Prelutsky. New York: Random House.

Rawls, Wilson. 1961. *Where the Red Fern Grows.* New York: Bantam.

Read-Aloud Rhymes for the Very Young. 1986. Selected by Jack Prelutsky. New York: A. Knopf.

Seeger, Pete. 1986. *Abiyoyo.* New York: Scholastic.

Sewell, Anna. 1877. *Black Beauty.* Maryland: Dennydale Books.

Small, David. 1985. *Imogene's Antlers.* New York: Crown Publishers.

Steig, William. 1976. *Abel's Island.* New York: Farrar, Straus & Giroux.

Tolkien, J.R.R. 1966. *The Hobbit.* Boston: Houghton Mifflin.

White, E. B. 1946. *Stuart Little.* London: Hamilton.

Zolotow, Charlotte. 1972. *William's Doll.* New York: Harper Collins.

Bibliography

Anderson, Richard C., and J. L. Hidde. 1971. "Imagery and Sentence Learning." *Journal of Educational Psychology* 62, 6:526.

Bell, Nanci. 1986. *Visualizing and Verbalizing.* Paso Robles, Calif. Academy of Reading Publications.

Borduin, Beverly J., and Charles M. 1994. "The Use of Imagery Training to Improve Reading Comprehension in Second Graders." *Journal of Genetic Psychology* 155, 1:115–18.

Brooks, Jacqueline, and Martin G. Brooks. 1993. *In Search of Understanding: The Case for Constructivist Classrooms.* Alexandria, Va.: ASCD.

Brooks, Jacqueline, and Martin G. Brooks. 1999. "The Courage to Be Constructivist." *Educational Leadership* 57, 3:8–24.

Bruer, John T. 1999. "In Search of Brain-Based Education." *Phi Delta Kappan* 80, 9:648–57.

California State Board of Education. 1999. *Reading/Language Arts Framework for California Public Schools: K–12.* Sacramento: California State Board of Education.

Campbell, Joseph. 1949. *Hero with a Thousand Faces.* Princeton, N.J.: Princeton University Press.

Chomsky, C. 1978. "When You Still Can't Read in Third Grade: After Decoding, What?" In *What Research Has to Say about Reading Instruction,* edited by S. J. Samuels, 13–30. Neward, Del.: International Reading Association.

Chugani, H. T. 1996. "Functional Maturation of the Brain." Paper presented at the Third Annual Brain Symposium. Berkeley, California.

Daniels, Harvey, Steve Zemelmen, and Marilyn Bizar. 1999. "Whole Language Works: Sixty Years of Research." *Educational Leadership* 57, 2:32–37.

de Beauport, Elaine. 1996. *The Three Faces of Mind.* Wheaton, Ill.: Theosophical Publishing House.

Diamond, Marian, and Janet Hopson. 1998. *Magic Trees of the Mind: How to Nurture Your Child's Intelligence, Creativity, and Healthy Emotions from Birth through Adolescence.* New York: Dutton.

Donnelly, J. 1987. *The Titanic Lost and Found.* New York: Random House.

Durkin, Dolores. 1983. "What Classroom Observations Reveal about Reading Comprehension Instruction." In *Reading Research Revisited*, edited by L. M. Gentile, M. L. Kamil, and J. S. Blanchard. Columbus, Ohio: Charles Merrill.

Emig, Janet. 1983. "Non-Magical Thinking." In *The Web of Meaning*, edited by Janet A. Emig, Dixie Goswami, and Maureen Butler. Portsmouth, N.H.: Boynton/Cook.

Escondido Union School District Board of Education. 1979. *Mind's Eye*, prepared by Marjorie Pressley, Margaret Horton, James Retson, and Wilhelmine Nielson. Escondido, Calif.: Escondido Union School District Board of Education.

Fielding, L. G., and P. D. Pearson. 1994. "Reading Comprehension: What Works?" *Educational Leadership* 51, 5:62–68.

Flippo, Rona F. 1999. "Redefining the Reading Wars: The War against Reading Researchers." *Educational Leadership* 57, 2:38–41.

Gambrell, L., B. A. Kapinus, and R. M. Wilson. 1987. "Using Mental Imagery and Summarization to Achieve Independence in Comprehension." *Journal of Reading* 30, 7:638–42.

Gardner, Howard. 1983. *Frames of Mind: The Theory of Multiple Intelligences*. New York: Basic Books.

Goodman, Kenneth. 1986. *What's Whole in Whole Language?* Portsmouth, N.H.: Heinemann.

Holdaway, Don. 1976. *Foundations of Literacy*. New York: Ashton Scholastic.

Johnson, Terry D., and Daphne R. Louis. 1987. *Literacy through Literature*. Portsmouth, N.H.: Heinemann.

Joyce, Bruce R. 1999. "The Great Literacy Problem and Success for All." *Phi Delta Kappan* 81, 2:129–31.

Kosslyn, Stephen M. 1994. *Image and Brain*. Cambridge, Mass.: MIT Press.

McCormick, Sandra. 1977. "Should You Read Aloud to Your Children?" *Language Arts* 54, 2:139–43.

McCracken, Robert A., and Marlene McCracken. 1978. *Reading Is Only the Tiger's Tail*. Winnipeg, Manitoba: Peguis Publishers, Ltd.

National Center for Educational Statistics. 1994. Data Compendium for the NAEP Reading Assessment of the Nation and the States. Washington, D.C.: U.S. Department of Education.

Olson, May W., and Thomas Gee. 1991. "Content Reading Instruction in Primary Grades." *Reading Teacher* 45, 4:298–307.

Osterroth, Peter H. 1993. "Optimum Mental Functioning." *Journal of Instructional Psychology* 20, 4:318–21.

Pearson, David P. 1993. "Teaching and Learning Reading: A Research Perspective." *Language Arts* 70, 6:502–11

Rose, Laura. 1992. *Folktales: Teaching Reading through Visualization and Drawing.* Tucson, Ariz.: Zephyr Press.

Samples, Robert. 1976. *The Metaphoric Mind.* Reading, Mass.: Addison-Wesley.

———. 1987. *Open Mind/Whole Mind.* Rolling Hills Estates, Calif.: Jalmar Press.

Sautter, R. Craig. 1994. "An Arts Education School Reform Strategy." *Phi Delta Kappan* 75, 6:432–37.

Schefelbine, John. 1995. *Learning and Using Phonics in Beginning Reading.* Scholastic Literacy Research Paper 10. New York: Scholastic.

Shanahan, Timothy. 1999. "Twelve Studies That Have Influenced K–12 Reading Instruction." *The California Reader* 32:16–23.

Showers, Beverly, Joyce Bruce, Mary Scanton, and Carol Schnaubolt. 1998. "A Second Chance to Learn to Read." *Educational Leadership* 55, 6:27–30.

Smith, Frank. 1999. "Why Systematic Phonics and Phonemic Awareness Instruction Constitute an Educational Hazard." *Language Arts* 77, 6:150–56.

Sylwester, Robert. 1982. Lecture on Brain Hemisphericity. Paper presented at Redding Reading Conference, Redding, California.

———. 1995. *A Celebration of Neurons: An Educator's Guide to the Human Brain.* Alexandria, Va.: ASCD.

Thompson, Ross A. 1998. "Early Brain Development and Social Policy." *Policy and Practice of Public Human Services* 56. 2:66.

Wolfe, Pat, and Ron Brandt. 1998. "What Do We Know from Brain Research?" *Educational Leadership* 56, 3:8–13.

Find More Ways to Make Learning Easy for Your Students

Bestseller

BEGIN WITH THE BRAIN

Orchestrating the Learner-Centered Classroom

by Martha Kaufeldt, M.A.
Grades K–6

A must-have for all teachers, *Begin with the Brain* provides brain-based learning methods for teaching and controlling the classroom in ways that make every student comfortable, ready and eager to learn.

1102-W . . . $32

MI STRATEGIES FOR KIDS

Featuring Brilliant Brain and Magnificent Mind

by Ellen Arnold, Ed.D.
Grades K–6

Meet the challenges of students' various learning needs. This set of 6 student books and an in-depth teacher's guide help assess students' strengths and learning difficulties. Whimsical characters introduce students to strategies for focusing or mastering tasks including reading, spelling, multiplication, and more.

Teacher's manual and one copy each of 6 student books
1140-W . . . $42

LEARNING VS. TESTING

Strategies That Bridge the Gap

by Pat Wyman, M.A.
Grades 1–8

Super spelling strategies, math mastery tricks, picture maps, and memory pegs are just a few of the tools to help your learners improve memory skills and comprehend the material better. These useful techniques help you teach in the ways your students learn to prepare them for the way they are tested.

1116-W . . . $29

THE MI STRATEGY BANK

by Ellen Arnold, Ed.D.
Grades K–12

Find the best ways to teach students who learn in many different ways in this handy resource. It is chockfull of quick, easy-to-implement strategies. For each of the multiple intelligences, you get lists of techniques to improve—

- Learning
- Reading
- Note-taking
- Writing
- Spelling
- Math skills

1099-W . . . $18

Find More Resources to Inspire Your Students to Explore Their Full Learning Potential

Bestseller
KID SMART POSTERS

by Donna Kunzler

Grades PreK–6

Help students understand and learn more easily by utilizing all their learning strengths. Everyone loves these brightly-colored, kid-friendly posters. Includes the naturalist intelligence!

9 full-color, 11" x 17" posters
1815-W . . . $27

BRAIN SMART POSTERS

by Donna Kunzler

Grades PreK–6

Teachers and students can explore the ways their brains work and ways to improve thinking.

8 full-color, 11" x 17" posters
1820-W . . . $27

I HAVE A CHOICE POSTERS

by Stirling Crebbs

Grades K–5

Make your classroom a tension-free, comfortable, easy place to learn. These captivating posters give students important knowledge of their ability to choose their own actions and responses. Posters display 8 character traits including honesty, respect, and others.

8 full-color, 11" x 17" posters and annotated bibliography of children's books to reinforce the good choice in each poster
1823-W . . . $27

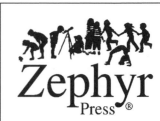